STARTING FROM THE BOTTOM

DR. ERIC L. CUNNINGHAM

PUBLISHED BY: WOM ENTERPRISES

Table of Contents

A MESSAGE TO PARENTS/GUARDIANS

DEDICATION

This book is dedicated in memory of Barbara and James Cunningham. They bought me into this world and I thank them for their countless sacrifices. I know they are the wind beneath my wings.

I also dedicate this book to my two beautiful daughters: Erica and Mallory.

They are precious jewels in my life and my total inspiration.

Acknowledgements

This book would not have been possible if it were no for countless mentors who poured themselves into me. With my deepest gratitude, I wish to thank every person in my life who touched me and taught me the valuable lessons that I have shared. Nothing is possible without the help of others. This book is the product of dedicated and trustful people who believed in me. Their lessons and support helped shape me to become the person I am today.

First, I want to thank Dr. Bertha Haynes. I met her over a year ago. She has passion for literacy and for helping others. I took a big shot and called her for help. I don't know why but I was led to contact her. After our first conversation, she didn't hesitate to help me write this book. She gave me the structure and support to make this dream a reality. For this I will always be grateful.

Next, I would like to thank my high school and college teachers. They saw the scholar in me. They demonstrated the necessary support for me to be successful. Without their unwavering support I would not have made it through the minefield laid before me. They were my angels quietly advocating for me behind the scenes.

Although I have many who supported me along the way, I want to especially thank Craig Seals, my high school Spanish teacher. He never once made me feel inferior. He always saw in me massive potential. He was a nurturing man who supported me. He also taught me the value of hustle points. Earning extra credit got me through his class. I have patterned my support for all children after him.

I especially want to thank Cham Pritchard my coach at Richard Bland College of the College of William and Mary. Coach Pritchard believed in me day one. I didn't have to prove myself to him. He *immediately saw the best in me and he proceeded to guide me to the next level. Thank you for all that you did for me. I will never forget all of the stories and lessons. You are a true friend and mentor.*

Sincere and special thanks go to all of my family and friends for their love, support and encouragement. They represent my army of righteous folks who always believed in me. They are my safety net whom I love dearly.

Foreword

For too long, our children have heard that it takes a village to raise a child, and for too long that adage has gone unheeded and watered down in meaning and example. And then comes Dr. Cunningham. In STARTING FROM THE BOTTOM, he gives credence to the meaning by drawing upon examples that teach and guide -- examples from the community of life.

Only a burning desire by one in the community to clearly guide our youth and show them how to navigate the challenges of their lives has helped create a pathway to potential success for them instead of having them flounder in despair and lack of direction. This desire is fostered by a community leader who gets his point across through personal reflections, historical and contemporary anecdotes.

It has been a privilege to work with Dr. C as he brought STARTING FROM THE BOTTOM to fruition and to learn many lessons during the process. And what I learned, our youth will learn. Young readers will learn to set lofty goals early in life and reach them through unwavering determination. They will learn that when they fall, they must not stay down but get up and try again. They will learn that every step on the stairway to an accomplishment represents a goal. They will learn that each person is a pioneer, a person who is willing to forge through obstacles and set a tone that enhances his life and that of others.

They will learn that every successful person that we know endured multiple failures but was not influenced or controlled by those failures. They will learn about life changing events and people who helped chart a new course and impacted the lives of others. Furthermore, they will learn self-determination from people they interact with daily, including coaches, teachers, and yes, even parents.

We share these lessons with you, the reader, as examples of what is possible from a leader who is willing and eager to cast wide his net of expertise. If you can see an image of yourself in just one of Dr. C's lessons, or if one of these stories is also your story, then the threads that bind us are strengthened. Dr. Cunningham shows that he has always been propelled by the knowledge of what he wanted and was determined not to quit until he got it. What resonated with me throughout the undertaking of this book was that he has a passion for motivating youth and that he is able to use everything as a teaching moment.

In addition, there is something here for every child who reads it; as a result, I'm hoping that every child who can will pick up this book and read it and reflect on the teachings that Dr. C so eloquently shares. But be aware that the advice and teachings imparted from STARTING FROM THE BOTTOM are not only relevant to kids but also to adults. Read it and that truth will be confirmed. While it serves as a partial memoir and reflection of Dr. C's life, STARTING FROM THE BOTTOM talks to and instructs youth and adults -- a careful reflection as it is read reveals that there is wisdom imparted to all who dares to read it. This is a brilliant talk to our kids – a talk they can relate to and never resent. It also resonates with our parents and other adults. Keep in mind though that it was intended for our youth, but any adult who reads it will be inspired. In fact, it can be a reawakening for adults who read Dr. C's views. Wise adults who are young at heart will find themselves re-evaluating their views of life and their assessment of the past.

This book talks about Dr. C's growing up years, his ambitions and determination to reach the pinnacle of success. It makes the reader think about life, where he wants to go and how he is going to get there. It gives advice that should be heeded and emphasizes that things that you want will not always come easily. What worked for Dr. C. can work for anyone with determination and resilience.

Importantly, for the young reader, it talks about failures.

Examples of failed opportunities and how Dr. C refused to let them negatively color his vision are shared. He emphasizes that failures give us the opportunity to try again and go back and prepare even more. He further emphasizes that if you fail at something you want, never give up. <u>Always</u> try again.

One last thing. Whether you are a young reader or a responsible adult, after reading this book - or while you are reading it – carefully reflect on and measure your own mental and professional growth. Confirm how you have made a contribution to our future champions. Further reflect on how you as a resident of a village help raise a child who can benefit from our guidance and support. How many Dr. Cunninghams do you have in your village?

Bertha Kenney Haynes, PhD
Rocky Mount, NC

INTRODUCTION

What I've learned in my life is that every person has one thing in common: we all have a story to tell, and the difference between those who are successful and those who aren't is how they handle the adversity. Whether they remain in control of the story or let someone else script the paper, every person has a story to tell and you have one, too. I am ready to share my story so that you will learn how I became the man I am today. Within these pages, I intend to teach you the strategies that you need to be successful regardless of your circumstances.

Sometimes those circumstances wrought pain. Many times, people believe they have a patent on pain because "my pain is worse than your pain." No, no, no! Pain is pain and we all experience pain. As we discuss circumstances, we are going to talk that how to conquer the pain, how to move past and through the pain and achieve success beyond measure.

I am going to share with you how I have been successful throughout my life despite adversity and the strategies I have applied that helped catapult me from the bottom to where I am today. You see, I believe that if I can do it, we all can do it.

I want you to enjoy this book. Sit back, take notes, and reflect on yourself as I open up and share with you what it takes to be successful. Keep in mind that you should not let your current, painful, challenging or normal circumstances dictate your future success.

As you read, you will see that I will share facets of my life, not just my professional life, but the spectrum of my life. I wanted to inspire others and how I got to be Dr. Cunningham, Superintendent of Schools. I am certain that in examining my life, you will be able to find similarities in your own life and, hopefully, those similarities will allow you to understand yourself even better and see how gifted you are.

I knew early on what I wanted to do with my life. I had an infinity for helping and inspiring young people, and it seemed to me that I could best do that by setting a lofty goal — I would be a school Superintendent. I pursued my dream and won.

According to statistics, expectations, what other people said, incorrect assumptions, the media, and articles in the newspaper, many people would say I should not be a superintendent of schools. My life's journey should have gone in another direction because (1) I am an African American male, (2) I was the product of divorced parents, and (3) I lived in poverty. But although there were people who told me I would not be successful, there were also a lot of people who told me I could accomplish my goal of becoming a School Superintendent.

You see, historically, there have always been unfair preconceived norms that African American men were born lazy, slow, and inarticulate. There was also the perception that we wanted handouts instead of hand-ups and that we were not willing to put the effort into really trying to become something. I want to dispel that myth. Yes, that is exactly what it is, a myth. Adherence to that so-called norm can be counter-productive and deter us from our goals, especially if there is a lack of spiritual intervention.

What I found is that through God's grace and intervention, I became a Superintendent right at a time I was supposed to and I was able to accomplish all the goals that led me to where I am today.

In addition to pointing out necessary strategies to become successful, this book serves as a road map. It is designed to provide a course for you to navigate, to inspire, and to give you a clear understanding of why it is important to have specific goals, unwavering faith, confidence, perseverance, and endurance. Life is going to throw you a series of ups and downs that are so powerful all of the wind will be knocked out of you. If you realize that you have what it takes, you will not be traumatized, but go on to master your craft. Even though you do not have money to achieve your goals, you will have experiences that are just as important.

My dad was a Vietnam veteran. He served two tours in Vietnam. He actually won medals. I always wondered how he could go to Vietnam twice in the 1960s and do well. You see, when he returned and retired from the service, the best job he could get at the time was that of head custodian. But you know, my father never ever complained about it. He just did his job and he did it with pride. And in watching him do his job, he taught me that education – he was a high school dropout, he didn't finish high school – he taught me that education was vital. *It was vital!* It was necessary to take you out of your current circumstances. And his dream for me was that I would utilize education, catch up, keep up and take the lead. He wanted me to chart a new course and create a path that was different from his.

It is my hope that this book will be interesting, informative, and inspirational. Look at my experiences that prepared me for where I am today and it will be useful to you. I want you to understand that I am going to share with you amazing stories that show perseverance and a strong work ethic. I hope that you enjoy what I have to say and find it useful as you aspire to live a five-star champion life.

Chapter 1
Create a New Path
#DreamBig

As I think about it, my pathway crystallized early on in my life. I began thinking of my pathway as far back at 10th grade. I want to talk about that and about some major obstacles in my life that I had to navigate around leading up to my associate's degree, my bachelor's, my master's, my education specialist's and my doctorate degree from the University of Virginia. It was not an easy road.

Graduating from high school was not an easy road. Making sure I had a marketable skill along the way was not an easy road, and I want you to understand that you need to make yourself valuable. I learned this early on and had reminders throughout my life. It's that value proposition that is crucial to success. How do you make yourself valuable so that a school will want to give you a scholarship, so you can offer your services? It's that value proposition that I'm hoping you'll learn from my experiences. And as you learn from my experiences, they will allow you to shape yourself in such a way that people will recognize your gifts and want your gifts to help them and their organizations. That is your calling – to be able to shape yourselves and allow that shaping to be a value proposition for others to utilize.

I have many different experiences in which I've had to reinvent myself from the early days when I was a custodian, cutting grass, shoveling the sidewalk when it snowed, bagging groceries, working in summer programs, working in construction . . . working in so many jobs, but at each level in each job, I was able to learn more about myself that I could transfer to the next experience.

I look at each of my life accomplishments as individual stairs with the staircase representing a series of goals. The staircase has no limit; each step represents an accomplishment. No matter how small the steps, always remember you are higher up on the staircase. The higher you go up, the view from that NEW position changes. What's unique is once your view changes, your condition will also change. Your likes and dislikes will change. Your circle of influence will change. You will change. You will notice that your strategy to get to the next step will change as well. What I have learned is to focus on the next step. So many times, we focus our attention on the top of the staircase and not the individual steps. When I lost focus on the next step, I failed to reach my short-term goal. The feeling I felt when I failed was misery and defeat. Sometimes I would fall back a step and return to a place I thought I was free from. So, don't lose sight on what is right in front of you! The next step is your best choice. The term I like to use is *incremental growth* which means step-by-step.

When you take the incremental approach, you focus on what it takes to make it to the next step, not the top. Here is an example: when you were in kindergarten why didn't you focus on graduation? I bet you are thinking a lot of possible reasons, right? You were so young you could not see that far into the future. What you could see was the first grade--the next step. When you passed to the first grade, your focus changed to not remain in the first grade but to be promoted to the second grade. You get the picture. Each grade brought you closer to the graduation. This is the incremental approach in action. The higher you climb, your view changes which, in turn, shapes your thinking. Your thinking changed because the requirements to make it to the next level changed.

In a lot of ways, I see myself as a pioneer, someone who is able to forge through obstacles and create pathways that change my entire life. I am the first in my family to graduate from college with a doctorate, and I am the first in my family to become a school superintendent. But in a lot of ways, I am not the first in my family to boldly go where we have not gone before. I want you to understand that you come from a family of pioneers as well. You cannot be who you are today unless you begin to recognize those who have blazed the path before you. Yes, you are a pioneer, but you are not the first pioneer.

So I set several goals in front of me. For example, the first goals were to earn a scholarship and play college basketball. I wanted to go overseas to play college basketball and to be able to play in the NBA. How do you do that when you don't make the SAT cut score and all schools withdraw their offers, but you still have a goal of going to college? How could I do that when I didn't even have the grades to be eligible to play college basketball? Once you know you would not and you weren't good enough to be invited to play, you're going to have to enter the world of work. How do you make that big step into the world of work? You see, I had to reinvent myself. How did I reinvent myself and earn an associate's degree and then get a college scholarship at Liberty University? I had to reinvent myself.

Slowly and surely throughout the course of my life, I've had to become different versions of myself, like different versions of the cell phones that are frequently upgraded and improved every few months. At the time I wrote this book I was fifty years old. I was version 5.0 or 5 reinventions of myself. During the journey to excellence, every circumstance and every step that I took changed my view and required that I upgrade my skills.

Everywhere along my path, I had to discover one thing: we all need each other. We are not isolated people; we are a community of humans. And, as humans, we need each other to survive. I have always found that I am better on a team. I am better working alongside others. We are a better community and a better neighborhood when we are all working together. And that is another purpose of this book: to show how we can all work together and forge our lives into a better place.

Now, as I reflect upon my life as Superintendent, I know that I am at the top level of the public-school educational arena and it is now time for me to share my 50+ years of experience and "pay it forward." As I look at my past experiences, I hope my journey will awaken the champion inside of you. I reached this level by focusing on each step along the path.

I believe that every person has a sleeping champion inside and that is why I have dedicated my life to becoming an educational leader to help awaken the champion inside of YOU!

Chapter 2
Strive for Five
#BeDetermined

If you were to Google *5-stars*, you would see many images, meanings and references. Five (5) stars is a ranking system: one star being the lowest and five being the highest. This ranking is applied to movies, positions and accommodations. I would like to apply it to life. To "strive" means you are making your greatest effort. When you "Strive for five," your greatest effort becomes your very best. You are willing to fight vigorously and endure whatever pitfalls may come your way. Every time you get hit, get back up. Why? Because you are striving and willing to endure whatever comes your way. You will not allow anything to deter you from accomplishing the top rank or "FIVE."

I am passionate about helping everyone live a 5-star life. I am passionate about instilling in everyone the three R's: Readiness, Respectfulness and Resiliency. You may not be the most talented person or the smartest person, but you can make a commitment to the three R's. And that is exactly what I would like you to do. My goal is to help everyone reach that top level of their personal staircase. You see, I believe all of us have a staircase and at the top of that staircase is where you are supposed to be. And my goal is to help you get to the top of your staircase of life. You can do that by embracing education, taking full advantage of education, taking education seriously, and doing the things that you need to do. Be Ready! Be Respectful! Be Resilient! (The 3 R's).

I don't want to break anyone's spirits. I want everyone to understand that through your spirit, you can always achieve excellence. So, I, through education, have always wanted to create an environment through which children love coming to school. There is nothing better than seeing kindergarteners running to school and seniors strutting across the stage to receive their diploma.

You have to love school and learning. So as Superintendent, I want that warm, loving, and nurturing environment for all young minds grades K-12 and beyond. I want your spirit to be strong so that you will be able to ward off all illnesses. Teachers are very happy to help you be the best you can be. You just have to practice the 3 R's and follow the roadmap that is laid before you.

I believe this is the *strongest* country in the world. I believe this is the *best* country in the world. I can remember when I was in tenth grade and I was down: I was cut off the basketball team. I can also remember a teacher coming to me and saying, "Eric, you got dealt a raw deal. You are a good guy and you got dealt a raw deal. She went on to say, "I want you to understand that although you got dealt a raw deal, you live in the most powerful country in the world, the United States of America, and the United States has a foundational belief; that is, if you work hard with a laser focus, you will be able to plant something that grows and you will be transformed through your work ethic. What you plant, you will reap."

What she planted in me that day was a powerful lesson for a 10th grade student. I said to myself, I will persevere, I will not give up and I will be successful. And it actually happened every step of the way. So, I want to pass those same words to you: "What you plant you will reap!" In fact, you will be more than successful. You will be actually transformed into something brand new, and people will love you for it and gravitate toward you.

So, let me share some of Dr. Cunningham's insights for creating a new path:

- **I want you to be honest and ethical.** I want you to conduct yourself with integrity. Integrity is having strong moral principles and values. Say what you mean! Mean what you say! I want you to speak up for yourself against all types of injustices. Whether you have been mistreated or abused, or have things gnawing in your stomach, learn to speak up for yourself.

- **I want you to appreciate working on a team.** I want you to understand that just like the fingers on you hand, each finger is weak, but when you ball these fingers into a fist, they become strong and you will have more power. I want you to know that working together as a team is the most powerful force in the world.

- **I want you to know that there will always be people that will try to deter you from your dreams**. You are going to learn to separate them and remove yourself from them. They see things in you that they wish they had, and their only goal is to keep you from achieving your dream.

- **I want you to understand that you don't need to worry about the past.** There will always be negative circumstances in your past which may keep you from selecting new goals. Don't allow people or events of your past to control your present-day thinking. Whatever your past pains are, you must learn to let them go in order to expand your present growth.

- **I want you to focus on the here and now.** Be aware. Live in the moment. Be appreciative that you are alive, and because you are alive here today, you have a fighting chance.

- **I want you to surround yourself with people who have your best interests in mind.** You might not like what they have to say to you, but they are saying it to you in the spirit of love because they want you to recognize that there is something better in you and they can see what you can actually become. So, I want you to seek out those angels around you for advice.

- **I want you to believe in community service.** I want you to always believe it is better to "Pay It Forward" and help people out; be polite and kind to people and demonstrate a sense of gratefulness in everything when nice things are done for you. For example, say "please" and "thank you" to express gratitude.

- **Be confident!** When you are confident in yourself, and trust in your abilities, it is extremely hard for negative thoughts and negative people to enter your space. And finally.....

- **I want you to believe in yourself and understand that there is a place where inspiration comes from.** Believe in yourself and know that you can just *stick-with-it.* If you can just plant it in your mind and believe it in your heart, it *will* happen.

Chapter 3
Failures Are Your Best Lessons
#Don'tQuit

When I started playing organized basketball, I was in 10th grade and attended Thomas Dale High School in Chesterfield, Virginia. To a lot of people, I was a late bloomer. I was tall and athletic but not very good. So, you know, I could make do. When I tried out for the team my 10th grade year, I had never played organized basketball, just street ball – street ball on Sundays. Each neighborhood in the area had a basketball team. Many of the teams consisted of grown men who once played high school or college ball. So, Sundays were the main event. Spectators would show up with their coolers and music and cheer for their teams. I had worked my way up from that street team.

I finally decided to try out for the high school team. In eighth or ninth grade I couldn't have played because I didn't get my physical in time: my mother was unable to take me to get my physicals, and at that time, we didn't have physicals in school. If you had to go to the doctor and the coach didn't know you, you couldn't go to the doctor and get your physical. Anyway, I go and try out. The tryouts lasted for three days, and I played with my team. I rebounded; I encouraged my teammates and tried to be that total team player. I was really proud of myself and for three days, I really made a mark for myself. I really stood out!

On the third day I went into the gym (the night before I couldn't sleep) and looked at the wall. To my surprise, I did not see my name listed on the team of 12 players! (My name was not listed because it was JV.) I looked at the list again and I didn't see my name. I actually ran my finger down the list, but I didn't see my name. I was shocked, actually shocked! You know, that was the first crossroad in my life. What was I going to do? Everything – my whole identity – was wrapped up in playing basketball, and now basketball had been taken from me. What was I going to do?

The other players who got cut said they actually felt better. They said, 'Well, if Eric got cut, I knew I wasn't going to make it.' They actually felt better about it, but – for me, like I said, basketball was my identity! It was the only thing I ever thought I was good at. And also, I knew that if I didn't get a scholarship, then I wouldn't be able to go to college.

I also knew that I was shackled in four areas: those four areas that shackled me were hopelessness, poverty, illiteracy, and fear of untrue beliefs. Signs of hopelessness were all around me. I lived in a tough neighborhood and crack cocaine was running rampart. All my friends and mentors were going in and out jail. And then at Friday night football games, you would see people standing together talking about 'back in the day.' Some were working, but we were all living in government housing. We didn't talk about purchasing a new home. We just wanted to survive. Those are the shackles of poverty. My mother was a single parent who worked hard. She worked two jobs. We all worked. I was doing things all around: I was shoveling snow in the winter; I was delivering newspapers; I was cleaning up the Laundromat and she was cleaning houses. We were poor. We would go to the free clinics for health care and to the free dentist for dental care. Then we would have to get clothes from the Goodwill. And stand in line for that big block of cheese. Although I could read, I wasn't reading on grade level.

I couldn't comprehend. When you cannot comprehend you tend to believe what you are told. This opens the door to fear and disbelief. Those were the four horsemen that had me shackled, so when I really tried to step out and do something with myself, fear and disbelief would step in. I would act out: nothing major, just minor stuff like being late to class, not being prepared, and being the class clown. But one day something happened! A teacher who knew my character and value came to me. She knew that I never got in big trouble at school. I was never a hard student and I never carried myself in a thuggish way.

My favorite actor at that time was Will Smith: a favorite rapper who went by the name of the Fresh Prince. I aspired to emulate him and applied his joyful spirit to myself. What I was doing was patterning myself after him. The next year when I returned to school, I was more likeable and friendlier. This was my first reinvention.

The teacher who came to me was a source of inspiration. All that she said resonated in my spirit. After all, I could not forget that my father served two tours in Vietnam and came back home with a Purple Heart. That, too, resonated in my spirit. That teacher also said to me, "You are an American and you need the work ethic of hard work." Although I can't remember her face (she was my Fashion Merchandizing teacher), I remember how she made me feel, and that feeling resonates in me today. That is why I am now Dr. Eric Cunningham. After those inspirational words from her, I began to really sit back, pay attention to opportunities and work especially hard. That same teacher then went on and helped me get a job as a bagboy at a grocery store. I was always working, but she went up there and vouched for me, making it possible for me to get a job at the local supermarket bagging groceries. I would always be able to go to work and also help my mother.

Chapter 4
The Value of Hard Work
#GoForIt

I tried several things to keep myself busy. If I wasn't playing basketball – and basketball was taken away – I knew I had to stay busy. I even tried to wrestle. Can you imagine my little 145-pound frame in that tight wrestling suit? I looked like a toothpick in tights. I even ran track, but I wasn't good in track. *I loved basketball.* I was definitely too skinny to play football. So, I just stayed busy.

The teacher in high school who got me a job at the local grocery store made me promise to start studying and working harder. She believed in me. When she came through for me I felt accountable. I didn't want to disappoint her. I started working, studying really hard. As the year went on, others began to notice my efforts. It was during this time that teachers really started to get to know me for themselves. It was 1982. Schools were not too long ago integrated. There were plenty of barriers that were laid in front of me. But the teachers really started to pay attention to my hard work and behavior change. Many offered to help me after school.

I did whatever I could to get back and forth to school. I built a bicycle, a 10-speed bicycle, and I would ride that bicycle sometimes to practice when I could not find a ride. The year I was cut from the team, I joined the marching band. I needed to get back and forth to practice and to participate in the games. I would do whatever I had to do. This is hard work and perseverance in action. You have to be resilient because every time you get knocked down, you have to get back up again.

I remember when I was not playing basketball. It was a year of transition. I remember when I was in the marching band and my mother was unable to take me to practice and to the band concerts. She had to work and I didn't have my driver's license. Part of the final exam was being at the band concert. I got on my bike fully dressed in my uniform and rode it all the way to where the band was performing. By the time I got there, the concert was over. I had failed the exam. I just turned around and went back home. I got a D in Marching Band that semester. Because Band was an elective, you should be making an A. So, young champions, you are going to be hit with a lot of tough, hard body blows that are going to knock the wind out of you, but you have to understand that through resiliency, you will be able to get right back up again.

I kept working in high school. My tenth year ended and I ushered in my junior year. I learned a lot. I grew up into a young respectful man. I acted differently. I was focused. I had reinvented myself and that reinvention was the beginning of understanding to let loose of the fear inside of me. For example, I had to become a better version of myself to get on that basketball team. I was a basketball player. I tried everything else but to no success. Those failures taught me a valuable lesson. As a result, I changed for the better and was selected for the team. You see, I knew what I needed to do and my thoughts never drifted from it.

I made better grades, and I was active in the student body. I had also made some new friends and I kept practicing with players better than me. During this time, as I stated earlier, teachers were very supportive of me. My Fashion Merchandizing teacher was special, but I can also remember other teachers. One of them was my Spanish teacher. I was in his Spanish 1&2 classes and he would always encourage me and pull for me. I also had a passion for history. My history teacher gave me all the necessary positive strokes I needed to excel. Because of her help, I ended up scoring the highest grade in the average class for the junior year and that catapulted me to honors government my senior year.

Can you imagine me, someone with four F's and two D's my freshman year, going to Honors English? But it all goes back to that Fashion Merchandizing teacher who told me, 'You are an American.' She also gave me other tidbits. She said, "Eric, you need a place to study. I know there is a lot of noise where you live, but you have to learn how to deal with it, so find a place to study and learn to be on time.

When I got my job at the local grocery store, I bought two things: I bought this executive style desk and a watch, a Seiko quartz watch. I paid thirty-five dollars a month until I paid that off. And can you imagine a banker's desk coming into the projects and my mother looking at me like *What?* It was absolutely beautiful, and it was so big that my brother actually had to use that desk to get on his bed. (We slept on bunk beds and it just took up a great part of the room.) With that desk, I was totally focused on my work.

So, what was happening? I was re-inventing myself. My brain was expanding and I was growing. I continued to practice and I continued to study. If I wasn't practicing and studying, I was working, but I kept going. (Young Champions, when this happens, you are becoming a better version of yourself. Keep going.)

When my junior year rolled around, I made the team! I had never played organized basketball before. I can remember the game against Colonial Heights. I had not played so I still did not understand all the rules of the game – I'm a street ball player and I wasn't a part of the rotation. But in that game with Colonial Heights, I was on the bench and the other players had fouled out, so the coach looks at me – I was probably the eleventh man – and he says, "Eric, get in there!" And I got off that bench and I was like *Wow, I can't believe I'm in the game! I'm finally in the game!* But I was a little nervous and I made some mistakes, but eventually the game actually slowed down. But I got it!

You have to remember that in a game you get one shot. What are you going to do with that one shot? You are going to make it work for you. And that is why you have to plan, to prepare, to train and to study. When that one shot comes, you want to be ready. When my one shot came against Colonial Heights, I ended up scoring 15 points for that game and the rest is history. The team belonged to me! The team belonged to me!

I kept playing my junior year, and during my senior year, I was captain. Also, I was in two honors classes and made all regions, all district. I led the region in scoring. I had a good career at Thomas Dale High School. I also had great friends that served as angels along the way.

Something catastrophic happened to me around that time: Len Bias died. And when Len Bias died, he was the greatest player I had ever seen play. I mean, he was an awesome player. He had suddenly died from a drug overdose and that actually changed my life in so many ways because I worshipped him. He was the man. You definitely know the man in your position and he was the man and his death saved my life. It made me focus and become more aware of my choices. It also got worse. The NCAA ushered in new rules – new qualifications to play college sports. For those who didn't qualify you were labeled Proposition 48. I could not score the minimal score on the SATs and I wasn't an All-American, so colleges would not sacrifice a scholarship on an athlete who couldn't play his first year. What do I do? I recalled my tenth-grade year in basketball. Now, I've cleaned myself up but I'm hit with another crossroad. What do I do? What do I do? You persevere. You look for another door.

A friend told me about a school called Richard Bland College of the College of William and Mary, located in Petersburg, Virginia, which is a junior college. So, I go there and meet the coach, Cham Prichard. I knock on Coach Prichard's door, he answers the door and I introduce myself, "Coach Prichard, I am Eric Cunningham." And he says, "I KNOW who you are." I led the team in scoring for the two years I was there and was MVP my second year. Each step you study, you prepare, you plan, and are ready for that one shot. I knew it was coming. I had been in these types of situations all my life. My one shot at Richard Bland came when we were to play Fork Union Military Academy. They were a nationally ranked prep school. Back in those days, there weren't many prep schools.

I remember Fork Union arriving. They ranked #2 nationally. In fact, their starting 5 went on to play Division 1 basketball. We had six players, all walk-ons. Talk about a David and Goliath match up! This was my one shot. I knew scouts were watching them so I needed them to see me also. I exploded and had the best game of my career! After the game, reporters were asking me about my remarkable play. The opposing coach was impressed. He commended my play. Those accolades opened up the next door for me to go to play basketball at Liberty University. I am so grateful for having that door opened up at Liberty. So, I leave Richard Bland with an Associate's degree and then I move on up to Liberty University where I played for two more years.

We go through life with these battles, but we have to have that strong work ethic where we continue to train *every single day.* I say that because I want you to realize that you are a miracle. We are all miracles, and I want you to understand that you were not born by chance. You have a purpose. So, it's a miracle that you are even here on this earth.

Think: As a result of all of that, all of the opportunities and accomplishments are supposed to come your way because you are a miracle. Many people are playing and wishing to hit the lottery. The truth is you have won the lottery. *You are the winning ticket.*

Chapter 5
Practice Everyday
#StayFocused

I learned early on, especially in high school, that the probability of being drafted into the National Basketball Association (NBA) form a small college was highly unlikely. I also had another problem: I had bad knees, so my physical capabilities exacerbated my chances. My knees started hurting me early in high school and I just knew that my body would not be able to keep up. In addition to that, I went to a small school and that diminished the odds even more. So, when I looked at the chances of going pro, I knew that I had to begin to prepare myself.

I learned coming out of high school that I needed to have an alternative plan. I wanted to leverage my basketball to catapult me out of poverty and into a better life. I knew I had to learn to use the gifts that I had. My gift was basketball and I marketed it to a school. My plan was to allow the school of my choice to utilize me, but, in turn, I intended to use that school to get my degree.

While at Richard Bland, I was looking for that one shot. I trained and practiced really hard as I kept my sight on my ultimate goal. That one shot came when I was playing basketball. My prowess in basketball opened the door at Liberty University. At Liberty, I played as hard as I could. Still I sensed I had to continue to face some physical challenges: my knees were taking extreme wear and tear. As a result, I began to focus more academically.

Coming from Richard Bland, I had a good foundation, so I went directly into my major. When my eligibility ran out, I graduated. I didn't have to come back for summer school, so if the coach changed his mind and said he needed the scholarship money for something else, I was good. I was free and clear and that was something I have been extremely proud of.

Athletes, do you really need to pay attention to the chance of going pro? Remember: This may not happen. The chance of your being successful is even greater because you have developed an alternative plan. And you need to have a plan, something you can rely on. That is the key. I was able to do that at Richard Bland and at Liberty University. One skill that I am extremely proud of is being able to adapt and leverage my own abilities to my benefit.

My competitiveness that I gained while playing team sports really gave me the tools to be the administrator that I am today. I learned to keep an eye on the team. In basketball, you have five people on the floor and each person has a particular role. In my role, I was a forward and that meant that I needed someone to feed me the ball. I might be roaming but I needed someone to feed me the ball. I might not be able to dribble the ball and take shots like the other players; I just needed someone to give me the ball. So, I had to rely on a teammate in order to be effective. That reliance and that appreciation for my teammates taught me gratitude for those teammates and gave me something that I can utilize in my present position today.

I am very, very appreciative of the team and the teamwork that goes into winning. But I want you to understand that a championship is not just a championship in sports. As superintendent, I have reached a pinnacle of my profession: a superintendent of education. That is the highest you can go. That is the major league. And that is exactly how I want you to look at your life. Ask yourself, "how do I use my skills--my basketball skills, my football skills, or my sports acumen as a leverage to obtain a full scholarship?"

These skills are essential: learning to play with your teammates, learning to work with each other, forgiving mistakes, letting things go, putting things behind you, and practicing every day. Remember that yesterday doesn't count. And don't worry about tomorrow. All we have is today, and today you must practice. You must continue to practice and then when that one shot comes, you will get in the game. When you finally get that promotion or that job, you will know that you are ready.

Chapter 6
Use Your Failure as Stairsteps
#Elevate

I have learned throughout my 50 years on this earth that life is going to throw you a series of curves and sometimes you are going to get hit so hard that you will actually lose all of your steam. Sometimes you are going to feel like giving up. I know because I've been there, but guess what: it's going to continue to happen throughout your life.

One thing about living is you get to listen to the wisdom of people older than you. I remember my grandmother used to tell me about circumstances. She said to me once, "Eric, you just have to keep on living." I pondered on that over and over again. What I've learned is that life is pretty much about ups and downs. You are going to have highs, you are going to have lows, you are going to have peaks, and you are going to have valleys. And guess what, those peaks and valleys are actually signs of life.

Every time you have a failure, there is an opportunity to grow. Opportunities are circumstances that make it possible to do something. Opportunities present situations which allow us to achieve our goals and become successful. There were particular failures in my life that allowed me to become the person I am today. The failure (opportunity #1) in my life that I believe was a life-changing moment was when I failed fourth grade. You see, I had a reading problem. I had a reading problem and I just didn't do well in school until I began to work hard to get that problem resolved. I can remember having so many F's on my report card that I would actually try to change them to A's. And I remember probably counting up to 16 F's on my elementary report card. Unfortunately, I was not a very strong reader, and I couldn't comprehend the text. I could read it, but I couldn't comprehend it. I could not mentally grasp what the words meant and be able to discuss and understand the meaning. If you cannot comprehend something, you cannot understand it. I had a reading disability. When you are performing in school at such a low rate, you end up being held back. And there I was. I had to repeat the fourth grade. Instead of being in the class of '83, it turned out that I ended up being in the class of '84.

The second failure (opportunity #2) in my life that I believe was a life-changing experience was getting cut from the 10th grade basketball team. As I stated earlier, I tried out for organized basketball during my tenth-grade year at Thomas Dale High School. During that time, I really felt like I was the best athlete, but I wasn't the best person I could possibly be. Also, being cut from that basketball team made me do a lot of self-reflecting and a lot of looking inward to see what needed to change. You see, I knew that I had to take responsibility for myself.

The third particular crossroad or failure (opportunity #3) was when I was ineligible to play collegiate basketball because of my low GPA and poor test scores. When I did finally pick up steam from being cut from the basketball team, I had to face that my Grade Point Average (GPA) was low. And even though I was doing much better my junior and senior years, my grades during my freshman and sophomore years had been D's and F's. Unfortunately, even though I had turned them around my junior and senior years, I could not pull up my GPA to the minimum cut score. Additionally, I couldn't make the Scholastic Assessment Test (SAT) cut score which is a requirement for being accepted in colleges and universities. I was labeled Proposition 48, which meant that I had to go to a junior college before entering a university.

When you are at a crossroad, you need to go left or right. Left, meaning the road to responsibility, or right, meaning the road to positivity. And you make the effort to take the right road and you talk about how this failure can grow you into a different version of yourself. You must see your failures as opportunities to find a new direction and create a new plan and a new goal. Never allow your failures to defeat you. I've always looked at every one of my failures as different versions of myself.

In the next chapter, we are going to be talking about <u>how</u> to use your failures (opportunities) to your best advantage.

Chapter 7
Failures Are Opportunities
#CreateandInnovate

I now know that failures are not fatal. They are actually stepping stones to success. But you must let failures work for you. You know, failures have actually become my best teacher. They are the mirrors that have showed me my real face.

I have learned that every successful man that I have studied failed at one time. If you look up and read the story about Michael Jordan's failures, you'll find that in high school, he tried out for the varsity basketball team during his sophomore year but at 5'11" he was deemed too short to make the team. But, guess what, he kept on shooting. The following summer he grew four inches and trained rigorously and earned a spot on the varsity team averaging about 20 points per game over his final two seasons of high school. Jordan became the first billionaire NBA player in history. He was motivated and determined to prove his worth and turned his failures into success.

Failures tell you about your weaknesses, your shortcomings, your lack of preparation, and your lack of efforts. So, if you can manage to learn from your failures, you can definitely reach where you really want to go. Making mistakes is just part of living. It is not a crime and it is not something you should be disciplined for. The ability to learn from these mistakes is what separates us.

As you read, I want you to become aware of lessons that you should learn from every failure. You will also discover that when you try again and redouble your efforts, you will gain vigor, enthusiasm and courage. You will not only become more vigorous, enthusiastic, and courageous but you are also going to face failures with more strength, more wisdom and more resoluteness than you have ever had, and that is what is going to catapult you to your greatest effort.

When you look at the word "failure," what do you think it means? A close examination shows that you weren't prepared adequately, or you weren't competitive enough, or you didn't analyze properly. Failures not only tell us that we weren't prepared enough, but they also reveal our shortcomings and tell us the level of success that we are currently at. In addition, if we are honest with ourselves, our failures will give us the encouragement to try, try and try again and go back and prepare even more. That's what makes failures a steppingstone to success.

Every successful person on this earth has failed not once, but several times in their lives. But you know what makes them successful is that they have been able to analyze the issue they failed at in real perspective and then they get back up and try again with more zeal. And guess what happens – they exceed expectations. Failures should not be allowed to create frustrations. They should not make you desperate or disappointed. I want you to look at failures as fuel that will give you strength to fight back with fierce fortitude and invincible zeal.

When I was in seventh grade, we had to memorize a poem, and the title of the poem that I selected was "Don't Quit," written by Edgar A. Guest. It has inspired numerous people through the years. That poem has always been something that I held to since seventh grade. It actually talks about failure and how to rise above it.

Don't Quit

When things go wrong, as they sometimes will,
When the road you're trudging seems all uphill,
When the funds are low and debts are high,
And you want to smile but have to sigh,
When care is pressing you down a bit,
Rest, if you must, but don't you quit.

Life is queer with its twists and turns,
As every one of us sometimes learns,
And many a failure turns about,
When he might have if he'd stuck it out,
Don't give up though the pace seems slow,
You might succeed with another blow.

Often the goal is nearer than
It seems to a faint and faltering man.
Often the struggler has given up,
When he might have captured the victor's cup.
And he learned too late, when the night slipped down,
How close he was to the golden crown.

Success is failure turned inside out,
The silver tint of clouds of doubt,
And you never can tell how close you are,
It may be near when it seems afar,
So, stick to the fight when you are hardest hit,
It's when things seem worst that you mustn't quit.

So, when we look at failure and quitting, we have to really understand that the one who tried is always better off than the one who dares not to try.

Only a person who dares to try can have a chance at success. So, you have to go for it and when necessary, get back up again. When you get knocked down, get to one knee. When you get to one knee, stand up. Blessed are those who once failed and got up again. Failures make you capable of evaluating your shortcomings, purging yourself and encouraging yourself to reach higher.

Abraham Lincoln, one of the greatest presidents of all time, failed a lot. He never let frustration overwhelm him, but when faced with adversity, he fought with more determination and full devotion. As President of the United States, he led the country through the Civil War and the slaves to freedom. Mahatma Gandhi, the Hindu political, social and political leader, failed not once but several times, but was never daunted by his failures; he always tried again. Both of these leaders fought for the sacred goal of freedom and, as a result of their efforts, they obtained it. But it did not come easily. I've learned that nothing comes easily, and when things do come easily they really are not that satisfying.

When you want to succeed, you must be ready to pay a price for it. And that price means you have to be brave enough to face your failures and setbacks and stay persistent with your efforts until your goal is achieved.

The reasons for failures may seem staggering. They can make your head swim. That's only if you look at all your failures as one, collectively. But when you look at them individually, they will no longer be formidable. So, you can either be defeated or discouraged by failure, or you can learn from it and analyze it and the causes of it. I want you to remove failure and endeavor again with all your strength and energy. It will surely lead you to success.

So, remember that one of your greatest successes might take a failure. When you were a baby, you had to first learn to crawl. While you were crawling, you fell. When you first started walking, you would fall again, but every time you got back up again because something inside of you said, "Stand up." Every time you failed, you got back up again. That was that internal drive in you saying, "Get back up, get back up." That drive is in you because you are walking upright. And when you started walking, you then began to run. When you slowed down again, you rested, and then you started running again.

Failures are nothing but pathways to success. They give you clues, but they only give you the clues that you need to rectify your mistakes, and they tell you how to change your efforts and move in the right direction so that you can achieve success positively.

I want you, young champions, to understand that your greatest glory is not refraining from making mistakes or failing. Your greatest glory is getting back up again every time you fail. When you were a little child, you were subdued by failures. You did not want to get back on that bike because you fell off of it, or you may have lost a race, or you may have lost a favorite toy, or got in trouble at school. Those are just simple misfortunes and *young minds* will use those misfortunes as crutches and excuses. But a great mind is what you have! Learn from those mistakes and get back up again and learn to rise above them. We must face every adverse circumstance as its master and do not let failure master us.

Many men owe the greatness and the grandeur of their lives to their beginning failures. Remember that failures are nothing more than stepping stones to success.

Chapter 8
Keep on Training
#Practice

I am reminded that one of my favorite stories about success, failure and overcoming adversity is a story about the Tuskegee Airmen. The Tuskegee Airmen were a group of African American military pilots, fighters and bombers. They fought in World War II. Officially, they formed the 332nd Bombardment Group and the 477th Bombardment Group of the U.S. Armed Air Forces. The Tuskegee Airmen were the first African American airmen aviators in the U.S. Armed Forces. During World War II, black Americans were still subject to Jim Crow laws and those laws restricted the movement and the activity of African Americans. At that time, during World War II, the military was segregated, so those men were subject to discrimination, both within and outside the Army.

Before the Tuskegee Airmen even entered the Army, they were discriminated against. All black military pilots at that time were trained on a segregated base. In 1941 the entire world was at war. We were actually fighting a war on two fronts, the Atlantic and the Pacific. The black military pilots were not allowed to do their job because of discrimination and thoughts that they were incompetent. As a result, they just trained and were not able to fight. But finally, their one chance came and they were given an opportunity.

When the opportunity arrived, they were *spectacular and they did an awesome job!* They were so spectacular that people were wondering and asking, "Who are these guys?" They are called Red Tails, but who are these guys? They were known as the Red Tail Angels because they were very good at what they were doing. And they were able to get the men home safely. Everyone wanted to know why these men were so good. They never stopped training. They trained and studied for years waiting for their one-shot. When their one-shot came they were ready. They were spectacular because they used their time wisely.

Another awesome story that I'd like to share is a story about the 1963-1966 Texas Western Basketball Team. They represented Texas Western College, now known as the University of Texas in El Paso. They were coached by Hall of Fame coach Don Haskins. He made history by winning the 1966 NCAA Men's Division Basketball Tournament. But what made him unique was that he was the first coach to start an all-Black starting line-up to win an NCAA basketball national championship, a feat that many people didn't think was likely. In fact, they defeated Kentucky; the score was 72-65. The Kentucky team was all-White until 1965. And guess who was on that team – Pat Riley. After a team wins a tournament, they are given the opportunity to cut the nets down as a celebratory gesture. This did not happen for this team because they were discriminated against. But they did not let it stop them. No way!

Why do I share these stories with you? It is proof that if you keep training and learning and working to be the best teammate you can be, you will be ready for your one-shot.

Chapter 9
Keep Grinding and Stay Persistent
#Endure

"No great achievement is possible without persistent work."
(Bertrand Russell)

The greatest power all human beings have is the power to control our mind and direct it to whatever goals we want. When we inject positive energy into our dreams, they will be nurtured to fruition. They will blossom and grow until they are full of power and strength.

It is important to encourage students to hold on to their dreams, to focus their minds on what they want to achieve, and to create a plan to follow to see that dreams come true. But we must first have a plan. The future is limitless but requires a plan of attack – a pathway to success. And that pathway requires persistence. Persistence is probably one of the most admirable characteristics a person can possess.

When I look back on my past and my accomplishments, the one common thread between all of my processes is being persistent. I had to develop the ability to be determined and to achieve my goal regardless of the setbacks, regardless of those failures. That's a distinguishing attribute of those who succeed in life against the odds and those who don't.

When we talk about the capacity to set goals, we must realize that we all have the capacity to set goals. When we were crawling, we got up and started walking; after we started walking, we soon started running. And we set goals and actually had a plan toward success; yet even so, we must keep in mind that only a few people succeed. Do you know why? I believe that it is because only a few people stick to the work that's required to accomplish a goal. You have to stick with it! That stick-to-itiveness is called persistence.

Many people stop before they even get started, quit in the middle, or can't finish at the end. Sometimes there are three distinct pieces that control us. It's like when you're working out in the gym. You have a set of ten and the last three, 8, 9 and 10 are your hardest. If you stop at 7, you actually feel like a failure because you didn't do 8, 9 and 10. And that's because it's hard, it's uncomfortable and there's uncertainty: "I don't think I can do it. I don't think I can do it." You are also afraid and doubtful. When those doubts come in, they can terrorize you. They will prevent you from accomplishing your goal if you are not persistent. Keep in mind that you cannot allow your motivation to be zapped. To guard against having your motivation zapped, you must have a plan and that plan should have three simple steps.

Step 1: Focus your mind on what you want. You have to see the goal, see the end. If there is no vision, it will not happen. You have to write it down. You have to make it tangible. And you have to know and believe that you are worth it and understand your purpose. When you focus your mind and identity on what it is that you want, you have to actually identify what your wants and desires are. Ask yourself, what is it that I want? You can do this by simply asking yourself an open-ended question and by being still and listening until your inner voice tells you what you want to have or accomplish.

Step 2: Write it down. Write those desires down. No matter how impossible they might appear to be, you must write them down. Then you have to determine *why*. Once you ask yourself why you want this, you realize that that's the fuel for your motivation. And that's the deep interconnection that allows you to want to achieve or have that something – that goal. If you know why you are doing what you are doing, it gives you energy to keep moving. For example, I wanted to go to college. I wanted to go to college although I was ineligible because I didn't have the grades to go. I wanted to go to college and play division-1 basketball. I had a goal. I became motivated. I knew that going to college would break the bonds of poverty and change my life. So, I had the motivation. I just had to write it down and make it tangible.

You have to identify your wants, your desires and be able to speak what it is that you want to achieve. I want you to understand the reasons why you want to achieve what you want. So, when you begin to outline the action steps that are necessary, you will begin to see how you'll be able to achieve what you want. When you know how to get what you want, it makes it easier to achieve it. To know how means that you need to do some research, and that's called "work." Now the work is hard because once you envision your dream and realize it can happen, it's now time to get to work. Sometimes you are going to be dealt circumstances or situations beyond your control, but you have the ability to rise above them and make a better life for yourself. You are in the driver's seat and navigating the ride of your life, but remember that production requires effort, effort requires focus, and focus requires intention.

Step 3: Keep a positive attitude. The road to success is laden with booby traps and pot holes. It's not a smooth road. In fact, it's going to be extremely challenging, and that's why only a few people succeed. There will be many times when you are faced with uncertainty and you are going to get knocked down. As a result, you are going to feel defeated and think you are a failure. Furthermore, you are going to think you are weak, and you may succumb to negative thoughts of fear and doubt. But in order to develop persistence and eventually succeed in your endeavors, you must always maintain a positive mental attitude. You must keep your thoughts focused on taking action and staying the course to achieving your goal.

Avoid negative thoughts and feelings; for they will ruin your concentration. Negative thoughts will zap your strength. In order to keep your dream alive, you have to protect it. The path to accomplishing your dream will not be easy and it will not be without disaster. Once you can see your dream, you must continue to pursue it and work on it. And when your inspiration kicks in, you have to feel determined and find the ability to stay focused. That requires practice and training.

Realizing your dream does not happen by wishing it were true, or by being afraid to face your fears. Amazing things happen by not allowing errors. Remember that fear stifles your growth and limits your determination. Endurance motivates action which results in productivity. Also remember that one must study to make the grade; one must practice to make the team.

We all must have a group of like-minded people who have our best interests in mind. We have talked about mentoring and mentors. Those mentors are the people who can help you succeed toward your goal, but you have to choose carefully because you have to trust them as being part of the team. If possible, I want you to only choose those who can give you unbiased judgment and who have a positive outlook on life. A simple test is asking, is the glass half empty or half full? If it is half empty, they are not positive, they are pessimistic; if they tell you it is half full, they are optimistic. So you can't afford to waste your time listening to cynical advisors or haters and pessimists. Those types of people will only zap you of your energy and draw you down to their level and, eventually, you will fail.

Now the power to fulfill your dream is stimulated from power and persistence, so we have to develop that discipline and habit. If you are not capable of developing discipline and good habits, all of your goal-setting and planning will go to waste. You have to stick to it because discipline is the bridge between what you want and what you actually accomplish. There will be hindrances that will stop you from moving toward your goal. It might be tempting to just walk away, but discipline will keep you going. Every day you will come back to school, and every day you will do your homework. Upholding discipline will be the best habit of your life, and it will allow you to stay the course. There are things you will need to do:

- **You will need to identify your wants and desires.**
- **You have to ask and determine *why* because that's the motivation.**
- **You have to write it down.**
- **You have to outline what it is you want and create an action plan.**
- **You have to remain focused and develop a positive mental attitude.**
- **You have to be surrounded by people who are in your network.**

Everyone has a network. Networks are only a set of relationships and patterns that they create. What you do in your network determines the type and quality of communication, the likelihood of collaboration and how successful you are going to be. Some networks are good and some are bad. Consider some examples of a bad network. We all know what they are. I just want you to take the opportunity to examine your network and determine if it is helping you accomplish what it is you desire.

What is your role in your network? How successful are the few people in your network? And then, finally, you have to develop that discipline, those habits, and that stick-to-itiveness or persistence. Persistence pays off. Remind yourself and believe the following truth:

If my mind can conceive it and my heart can believe it, then I know I can achieve it.

Chapter 10
READINESS
#BePrepared

For me, it all started with the desk. That desk was where a teacher told me that I needed to prepare to study. What she was basically telling me was that I got dealt a bad hand, but I had to play the hand I'd been dealt because it was my hand. What was important was how I played that hand. She was talking about being ready. So, what is *readiness?* Ready is when you prepare yourself daily. When she told me to go and get a desk and study and get a watch to be on time, she was preparing me for readiness.

When I first started my journey, I was making an F+! An F+!!! This means I was failing. Big time! As I sat at that desk, it became a portal and the F+ turned into a D. And then I would go back and study again. And then the D turned into a D+. I would go back to my desk and study some more and then that D+ turned into a C-. And then that C- turned into a C+. Something miraculous started happening: the teacher began giving me hustle points. Hustle points are nothing more than extra credit. These are extra credit points in which teachers see you are making an effort and need additional time. The teacher then started to spend time helping me. So, I started earning these hustle points, and that C+ turned into a B-. And that B- turned into a B+.

When I earned my first B+, it was in History. I just about lost my mind because here I was a student who had earned F plusses now earning a B. It was an amazing and exhilarating experience! So anytime I sat at that desk, I was preparing myself to be ready by attempting to do my work. And that attempt at readiness benefitted me. Even though many times my work was wrong, it was the effort I was putting into that work that began to make the difference because that difference was marked by higher grades.

So young champions, what I want you to know is that you have to come to school ready. Even if your work is wrong, you have to make an effort to do it. Make an effort to bring something to school every single day. Far too often, we worry about how it looks, if it's right, if it's perfect, if it's wrong. No! I want you to put in the effort in preparation and study to show your teachers your desire to achieve. Make an effort to come to school prepared and ready. every single day! If you do, I guarantee you that your teacher will reward you by giving you extra time and extra credit. Those extra credits are the points you need to be successful in life. Readiness is the key in order to be successful, but if you are going to be ready in life, you must learn to be ready for your job, for your college, ready for anything because you understand that readiness is nothing but preparation. And preparation is the key to success!

READINESS ACTION STEPS:

❖ Have a designated place to prepare your work

I remember the desk I bought in high school. That desk was so big, it barely fit my bedroom, but it gave me power. That desk gave me a place to prepare my work each day and I felt like a king. If you do not have a desk in your room, find another designated place: the kitchen or dining room table, the basement, the library. The place I selected to study worked for me in improving my grades; however, everyone has a unique learning style and what worked for me may not work for you. The important thing to remember is to find a designated area to study every day. This will get you into the habit of studying and will keep you motivated to study. Your designated area should be a comfortable place, free of distractions (yes that means no TV, videos, cell phones). Again, there is no one best place to study, but you must find a special place that will promote positive results.

❖ **Spend time alone studying and preparing for the next day**

Designate a daily study time. Gather all of your materials before you get started. Make sure you have all your books, paper, notes, pens, pencils, highlighters and other supplies. Turn off your cell phone and television. If you need to use the computer during your study session, stay away from social media and email. During your daily study sessions, it is extremely important that you write down anything that you do not understand so that you can remember to ask your teachers to explain the next day. Study every day. The minimum study time should be one hour no matter what day it is. It may be hard at first, but each day you will find that it is a rewarding habit. Consider writing short notes that reflect important facts to remember. Avoid studying more than one topic at a time. Reading is not the same as studying. Remember, when I was in school, I could read, but I could not comprehend. I did not understand what the words meant. When you are reading, make sure you can comprehend what you have read. If you can't, ask for help immediately.

❖ **Organize your work space**

Having a clean space can help you focus and get your work done with much more concentration. Remove anything that can distract you from your work that isn't needed for your assignment. If you spend just ten minutes cleaning your space at the end of every day, you'll be able to maintain your new organized lifestyle. Making a to-do-list at the beginning of each day or week can make you feel more focused and motivated to continue your work. If you make a list of all the things you have to do, no matter how small, you will feel more accomplished when you check those items off your list and move on to the next task. Make time for breaks. This form of organization will actually help you stay focused and motivated to finish your work assignments. A good practice is to take a five to ten-minute break for every hour that you work.

❖ Stay Focused

Staying focused can help you accomplish almost anything, from studying for a test to finishing your work an hour early. Staying focused can help improve your life, help you listen to people better, and also help you come up with a solution to problems at a quicker speed. Stop checking your Facebook or phone every fifteen minutes. Read more. Reading tests your mind's ability to stay focused on just one task at a time and can improve your focus. If you're always flipping through the channels on your TV, constantly switching radio stations, or texting five friends at a time, you'll be slowly losing your ability to focus on just one task at a time. Set aside at least 30 minutes to an hour to read each day. You can read the newspaper, a novel, or a work of non-fiction. It doesn't matter what you read, as long as you focus on reading it well and avoiding distractions. Distractions are enemies of staying focused. Some examples of distractions you should look out for are: Texting, social media, E-mail, and friends who do not have your best interest. Don't procrastinate. Procrastination is the thief of time. Avoid delaying any of your activities by leaving things to be done for tomorrow, next week, or next month. Stop making excuses for not doing your work.

❖ Always have your work done even if you don't know how. This is how to get hustle points.

The key here is to try. Don't let fears of not knowing how to do your work keep you from trying. Your work may be wrong and imperfect, but it shows effort and that you tried to the best of your ability. Mistakes give you fuel to stop driving down "I Can't Street" to making a right turn onto "I Can Street" and driving straight towards "I Can and I Will Avenue". Mistakes give you the fuel to work harder and re-invent yourself. Your teachers will recognize your efforts and help you earn hustle points (extra credit). Sometimes, the fear of making mistakes can keep you from trying because you are so afraid of not doing well. Don't let this happen to you. Give yourself permission to mess up. I have made tons of mistakes in my life but I never gave up. Your teachers have made tons of mistakes. Making mistakes are a part of life, but if you give up, you never get to move to the next level.

❖ Don't be afraid to ask for extra help

> *"Don't be afraid to ask questions. Don't be afraid to ask for help when you need it. I do that every day. Asking for help isn't a sign of weakness; it's a sign of strength. It shows you have the courage to admit when you don't know something, and then allows you to learn something new."* *-Barack Obama*

Now let's think about this. Barack Obama, the 44[th]President of the United States, asked for help every day! That's powerful! Too often students will feel the need to ask for extra help but remain silent because other students will laugh and say unkind words. You cannot allow yourself to just sit on the sideline. You must get in the game. Have you ever thought that those who are laughing at you may need extra help as much as you, but don't have the courage to admit it? Don't procrastinate and think: "I'll ask for extra help one day." Remember this: "One day is not a day of the week." Don't be afraid to ask for extra help today and every day if you need it. When asking for extra help, always approach your teacher with respect. For example, you could begin by saying. "I appreciate you taking the time to help me. I am struggling with my work, and I sincerely want to improve. I need to know what it will take to do better."

❖ Be on time

In the movie *Drumline*, the band leader tells the band *"If you're early, you are on time. If you are on time, you are late."* This is a good practice to follow for always being on time. There should be rare occasions when you cannot be on time, but make sure you have a reason and not an excuse. For example, on the way to school, your bus had a flat tire and caused you to be late for school. This is a reason. An excuse for being late for school would be you did not get out of the bed in time to go to the bus stop and catch the bus. Being on time shows good character and it also shows that you are responsible and considerate of others.

❖ Be the best that you can be

Being the best possible version of yourself means being positive and striving to do the right thing at all times. Know who you want to be and be that person. Once you know who you want to be, make a plan to improve. For example, if you want to be a more patient person, come up with a plan to practice patience in stressful times, such as counting to ten. Prepare for success. Eliminate things that stress you out and slow you down. ***Be one step ahead instead of one step behind***.

Create routines for yourself that will help you be the best that you can be: prepare for the next day the night before, lay out your clothes or pack your lunch, stop making excuses, get your work done before any deadlines, pay attention in class. Keep in mind that the journey to being the best that you can be will not always travel a straight road. You will sometimes have curves, turns and roadblocks but this is all part of driving towards your destination of *success. Don't be afraid to be great!*

❖ Rest and don't worry. Let it go! You are ready!

Get enough sleep. Lack of not enough sleep can contribute to stress, which leads to worry. If you are going through a bad time, take comfort in knowing that everyone feels like this at some point. Don't let your worries about school cause you to be unsure of yourself. Let it go! Keep repeating to yourself: I have done my best; I have worked hard and I am ready. Just let it go! Be optimistic and love yourself. Believe in yourself. Have determination and dedication. Have faith in your abilities. Be confident that you have done everything possible to prepare yourself. Remember: yesterday ended last night; today ends tonight; tomorrow is a new day. Refuse to give up. When things get tough, you get tougher. Don't quit! Know that you are amazing! You are a *Winner*! You are ready and the best is yet to come!

Chapter 11
RESPECTFULNESS
#Honor

Now that I was ready, I had to learn to be respectful. Many times, people have preconceived notions about who you are or where you are from. You see, I grew up in the projects. The projects had this bad reputation, and when teachers looked at my name and address on the roll, they knew where I was from. He or she automatically assumed that I must be a hell raiser because of my zip code. Students, you need to know that your zip code does not define who you are. People who judge you based on where you live or the color of your skin are weak minded. Don't let their judgments define you. Remember there are many people who feel the opposite. They are cheering for you. They want you to be successful. I was not a bad student even though I lived in a tough area. I learned that I had to run a course that had a lot of obstacles. In order to succeed, I needed the help of others. I needed to learn to win others over. I had to learn to be respectful especially to people in authority.

Growing up I spent many hours watching and listening to adults who shared stories about their life and how they experienced ups and downs. I listened and gained confidence that I could do anything and be anything that I wanted to be. From an early age, I knew I wanted to play basketball, and I knew that I wanted to go to college. Along my journey, I learned that both goals would be a challenge, but by being respectful to my parents, teachers, coaches and other adults, I realized that they could see my potential and believed that I could accomplish anything. This core group of believers taught me that failures are pathways to success, and success always leaves footprints. Through respect, people began to see me differently. When I played basketball, I respected the coach by winning every sprint and by being early to practice. I respected my teachers by coming to school prepared. I was coming prepared so much that one teacher helped me get my first job at the grocery store. Being respectful has awards.

Respect is like an olive branch. And that olive branch opens the door for people to give you a hand up. Respectfulness is the key that opens that door. So, you need to learn to be respectful: "Yes ma'am", "No sir." There is nothing wrong with that. Opening a door for a lady, being quiet and following directions is the key. When a teacher asks you to put away your cell phone, put it away. Don't look at them and roll your eyes, just look at them and listen. Demonstrate respectfulness. That is the key to success.

RESPECTFULNESS ACTION STEPS:

- ❖ **Follow Directions on First Request**
  Following directions is an important skill to have in school and in life. If directions are not followed, our goals and outcomes cannot be achieved. Following directions exists in all areas of life: academics, playing sports, cooking food, driving and navigation, in the military, prescriptions, playing games. All successful careers depend on following directions: teachers, doctors, chefs, hair stylists, veterinarians, and many, many others. The importance of instructions is so you will know what to do and know how to do it right. You need to know how to follow instructions at school so you will get good grades, or if you have an important job like being a firefighter, you need to know what to do in order to save somebody from a fire and save your life as well. There can be a lot of penalties of not following instructions, like if you didn't follow instructions with taking your medicine, you could get sick. If you didn't follow directions on the food you were making it wouldn't turn out right. You could also get lost if you didn't follow the directions on how to get somewhere.

The key to following directions is to focus and listen. Some students have trouble paying attention, sitting still, and are getting constantly called out by the teacher. Learning to follow directions the first time they are given can channel your energy into becoming a better student. A good student is one that is prepared, active, safe, interacting, and helping. Following directions show that you are cooperative and dependable. Some teachers will be very specific about their directions, so make sure you follow all of them. This could mean specific ways to title your assignments, places to put your answer, or specific information to include in your answers.

If you aren't sure about those instructions, ask the teacher. While teachers say they want students to be creative, they really want students who can follow directions and do work the way they asked. Don't be afraid to ask for help when you don't understand directions. Learn from your mistakes. Don't see mistakes as personal flaws; failures are guidance in how to do better. Take notes. One great way to keep focused on the class topics and the lesson is to take notes. Don't worry about writing directions word for word, just try to come up with a list or an outline of the important directions. This will help you stay focused and you'll have something to refer to later. Some tips for following directions and remaining focused:

- Sit in the front row; it makes it easier to pay attention.
- If you didn't understand the directions, ask the teacher to repeat them.
- Do not sit with friends, especially if you usually get in trouble. Even if you're not a troublemaker, the act of not sitting with your friends reduces the urge to talk and mess around. If someone is trying to get your attention, tell them that you're not interested

- Don't bring distractions, such as cell phones or games to class.

No one is perfect; however, striving towards the skill of following directions will help with completing assignments by avoiding unnecessary mistakes. Make sure you know what you are supposed to do and make all efforts to understand each step before going to the next step. Directions give us motivations to create, learn, grow, and become better.

❖ Listen with Your Eyes

Look people in the eye when speaking. Maintaining eye contact is polite and shows that you are listening. Pay attention to what others are saying. Do not interrupt but show that you are listening by asking questions. Practice good listening skills. When it comes to conversation, what you hear is what you get. Listening is a skill we sometimes take for granted. How many times have you been in the middle of a conversation and suddenly realized that the other person had asked you a question that you didn't even hear? How often are you so preoccupied with your own thoughts in class that you tune out the instructor? It happens to us all, which illustrates the difficulty of practicing this seemingly simple skill. The better you listen, the more correct information you will obtain; the more correct information you have, the better decisions you will make. When listening to people, engage in the conversation and make eye contact so they know that you care about what they are saying. People who listen more are more observant and therefore more thoughtful and have a better understanding of things. Make sure you really are listening and not doing something else. Try to make sure you are completely focused on the person who is talking and not get sidetracked. Make sure you are making eye contact with the person, not someone else or something else.

❖ **Think Before You Speak**

Choose your words carefully. The words you choose to use are just as important as the message you will give. Try to learn to calm yourself down and think through your emotions before reacting to situations or people. This will teach you to be more mindful of your words. Make sure your comments are relevant and appropriate to the conversation. Don't stray from the topic – stay focused. Consider the information: Is what you want to say effective, necessary, accurate, timely, and appropriate? If you are just responding because other people are talking, then it's possible your communication is unnecessary.

You want what you say to have impact, not just make noise. Be thoughtful about your tone: How you say it is, in many ways, as important as what you say. Tone of voice can express sincerity, or it can show negative thoughts. When you think before you speak, put yourself in the position of the person you're talking to. How will what you're going to say make them feel? If people aren't actually addressing you, they may not want your opinion. Try to tone down how much you force yourself into conversations. Avoid insults or inappropriate personal references that will send negative results. Remember - this is about thinking before you speak. If you do not know what you're talking about, do not try to be convincing. It's okay to express an opinion, but make sure others know what you are talking about. To remind yourself to think before saying something, pinch yourself on the finger or somewhere discreet. If you develop a routine for answering a question, you will be less likely to say the first thing that comes to mind. ***Remember that you have two ears and one mouth for a reason. This means that you should be listening twice as much more than you are talking. It is more beneficial to listen than it is to talk.***

❖ **Apologize If You Hurt Someone**

Saying you are sorry — it's something we have to do occasionally, and it's often a painful experience. Knowing how to apologize respectfully and sincerely is a beneficial skill a person can have in the professional world as well as in personal life. Get your apology started on the right foot by saying something along the lines of "I'm sorry", or "please forgive me." *Apologize when you are wrong.* When you do mess up, apologize immediately and with sincerity. Express that you are genuinely sorry and make efforts to avoid the wrong behavior in the future. If you are truly a considerate person, you will know when to apologize because you hurt someone's feelings even if you didn't mean to do it. Show your willingness to change. The most important part of any apology is your commitment to act differently in the future. If you don't at least *try* to change, your apology will lack sincerity. Make a commitment to act differently in the future and stick to it - if you truly care about the person you're apologizing to, you'll naturally want to avoid hurting them again. Old habits die hard. Promising to change is one thing, but actually changing is another thing entirely. We've all done it - sworn that we'd change our ways, and then made the exact same mistake again. If you do, you'll need to make another apology, but be careful - too many insincere apologies can damage or even end friendships.

❖ Show Courtesy and Be Polite

Politeness is an important social skill that can help you show respect. You can be polite by offering a proper greeting and showing good manners with words and actions. Being polite does not cost you a penny; it just makes you a better person. Being nice makes people feel good and paves the way to good relationships! It also helps you get what you want since people are more inclined to help you if you're nice to them.

You never know when a word or a few sincere words can impact someone's day. Take time to be kind and say *Hello, Please, Thank you, Excuse me, I'm sorry.* Hold doors open for others. Let elders take your seat. Help your parents by doing extra chores. Avoid cursing and being vulgar. Avoid gross and inappropriate topics. Smile when greeting someone; this establishes a sense of friendliness. Address elders with respect by using "Mr." and "Ms." Avoid gossiping. A polite person does not spread bad information about others whether it's true or not. If others are gossiping around you, change the subject or just walk away. Practice random acts of kindness. Look for opportunities when you can help another person. When you feel like you are going to give an unnecessary comment, try staying silent. Staying silent gives you a bit more time to think about what you could say instead of blurting out something rude and getting into trouble. Learn to pay attention. This demonstrates to others that you value their opinions and what they have to say. When you show care for others, it shows that you can be trusted. If you see a person without a smile, give them one of yours.

❖ **Practice Random Acts of Kindness**

Random (having no definite reason) acts of kindness and good deeds are actions that you take by doing something nice. Random acts of kindness come from the heart and show that you respect and care for others. You do not expect anything in return when you do random acts of kindness; you just want to brighten someone's day. Random acts of kindness will help you be the best that that you can be. The possibilities for the things that you can do are endless and will come to you with little effort. Some examples are:

- Share a smile. Smiles are contagious. Smiles cost nothing! If someone is sad, give them a smile. If someone is mean, smile anyway. If someone has a problem, smile and listen and offer to help if you can.
- Give compliments. Compliments cost nothing! "Wow, you look great! I love your new haircut! Where did you get that new sweater? It is beautiful!" Don't just think it. Say it.
- Visit the elderly and listen to their stories. Many elderly people get lonely and having a visitor to talk to can make their day.
- Volunteer for something that you care about: a homeless shelter, an animal shelter or other places within your community that may need help.
- Pay it forward (if you can). Pay for the soda of the person in line behind you. Feed parking meters

that have expired so the person does not get a parking ticket. Pay for the next person's popcorn at the movies. Remember, no one asked you to do this and no one has to know that it is you. You don't want recognition and praise because it is your heart guiding you to be nice to others.

- Do something for family members before they ask. Wash the family car, do the dishes, mow the lawn.
- Thank friends, family and others verbally or by writing thank-you notes. Just think what it would mean to the custodian at your school if he/she received a note that said: "Thank you for keeping our school so clean. You are the best!"

Random Acts of Kindness! Expect Nothing in Return!

Random acts of kindness are from the heart and are given freely because you RESPECT AND CARE about others. The feelings that you experience is your reward. Being kind is powerful ......
TAG, YOU'RE IT!!

❖ **Don't Discriminate. Respect the Space of Others**

Being respectful means showing that you value the time and space of others. Take time to think about how others are feeling. To be considerate, you have to put yourself in someone else's shoes, to have tact and be kind and gracious. When in public, try to keep your voice at a normal level. Avoid taking up too much space. Look where you're going instead of texting and walking. Be considerate of the financial situation of others. Don't embarrass your friends by making them admit they cannot afford to do things. Don't discriminate. Be equally nice and respectful to everyone.

Even if you're nice to your friends and teachers, but you aren't nice to people who aren't cool or popular, you may not actually seem as nice as you actually are. Do not judge others by race, age, gender, sexuality, ability, or religion. Be kind to people you see throughout the day that aren't always treated with respect. For example, homeless people are often overlooked or treated rudely, but they deserve the same respect and courtesy as anyone else. Respect differences. Be respectful to people who are different from you, even if you don't understand the differences. The differences among us are what make life interesting, and besides, you probably have more in common with people than you know. Even when you really don't see where someone else is coming from, be courteous and civil. You don't have to *love* everyone you meet, and you certainly don't have to agree with them, but you can still show them respect. Be respectful of people's cultural differences. Be respectful of people with different religious beliefs. Be respectful of people with different politics from you. Be respectful of players on the team that rivals yours and fans of the other team.

Don't be two-faced. Do not brag too much. Don't talk about people and don't be a backstabber. Being nice to others helps you gain their trust, and you're betraying that if you talk about them behind their backs. Remember to always treat people the way you would like to be treated. When you fully respect others, then automatically more people see you as nice, caring, trustful, and considerate. At the end of the day, you want to be respected for your views, ideas, and passions, even if the other person doesn't share them. You should offer the same courtesy to others as well. Treat others the way you want to be treated. Don`t judge other people with your standards, because what is good for someone can be bad or hurtful for someone else. Never resort to insulting someone during an argument. Don't let "I don't agree with your view on that" escalate to "You're an idiot." If necessary, stop the conversation before things get too out of control and you say something you'll regret. You're not going to get anywhere by disrespecting the other person; you'll just make a new enemy.

Chapter 12
RESILIENCY
#GetBackUp

To me, resiliency mean when we fall down, we get up. When we practice resiliency, we recognize that in life we are going to get many blows that will knock us down. Those blows will hurt and will knock the breath out of you.

There were many blows in my life: When my parents were divorced, when we were evicted from our home and we had to move to the projects, when I didn't get anything for Christmas. Those were blows. When the teacher accused me of cheating, and I hadn't, when I was cut from the 10th grade basketball team simply because the coach didn't believe in me. These were all blows. At times when life throws you a curve and you are faced with a crossroad, you are going to accept it or you are not. But you are knocked down! What are you going to do? I want you to be resilient. I want you to get back up again. I want you to get back up again! And when you are not flat on your back, you get up on one knee, and then you get up on the second knee. And then you get up on one leg at a time. And eventually you are standing tall.

Being resilient means the ability to bounce back from failure. You might feel depressed or upset with yourself. You might feel like giving up. But with resilience, you strive to be better (#optimism), you believe in yourself (#confidence), you have a plan for how to improve (#creative goals).

Resiliency, Endurance, Triumph: That's the whole purpose of this book. The race is not given to the fastest or always to the strongest; many times, the winner is the last standing. Endurance and resiliency are keys to climbing the staircase of success. When you fall, you get back up again. You learn to be the first to help your teammate; you help your brother or sister. You never stay down. You never stay down!

RESILIENCY ACTION STEPS:

❖ **Build strong character**

> *"Character is what you know you are, not what others think you have."*   *-Marva Collins*

Sometimes other people can make you feel embarrassed and humiliated.

Your "suppose-to-be" friends, classmates, and yes, sometimes teachers will sometimes say cruel words that are hurtful and make you feel sad: Do you think you are the only one who has had to wear used clothes? Do you think you are the only student who lives in the projects? Do you think you are the only graduate who cannot afford a cap and gown? But if you have confidence in yourself and determination, you are going to be something special. **It does not matter what others think. *It does not matter what you wear, what your zip code is, or how much money you have, but it's what's in your heart that* counts. *This is your character.*** When you fall down, character will allow you to get back up.

Some excellent ways to build good character are:

- Surround yourself with people of high character. Identify people in your life that you respect, people who you think have desirable character traits. Decide what you want to be like, what makes the best version of yourself, and find people with those strengths.
- Hang out with people who are older than you. Elders are also deserving of extra respect. Respect your parents,

grandparents, and other elders in the community for the valuable wisdom they have to share. As a young person, make it a goal to befriend someone much older than you and learn from them. Spend time with older relatives, talking and learning.

- Hang out with people you admire. The best way to build character is to hang around people you admire, who you want to be like, and who you can learn from. Talk to powerful people you want to model yourself after.
- Get out of your comfort zone. Building character means learning how to handle tough or uncomfortable situations. Volunteer helping at-risk kids after school, or spend time working in your community. Commit to difficult projects at school or at home and commit to doing them the right way. Learn to push yourself toward success, handle coming up short, and become a better person regardless of the outcome.

Have faith in yourself. Believe that you can do whatever you put your mind to. Know that if you fall down or make a mistake, it is not the end of the world. Mistakes happen and people fail sometimes, but it is how we learn from these mistakes and failures that make us who we are and help us build character. If you want to take control of your life and develop good character, learn to always think about doing what is right. This is your Character.

Don't come up with reasons to not do things.
Look for reasons to act!
Don't invent excuses, invent reasons!

❖ **Be optimistic**

Being optimistic means being positive, hopeful and confident. An optimistic person sees the glass as half-full instead of half-empty. In situations where life gives you lemons, an optimistic person will find sugar and water and make lemonade. Being optimistic helps you learn from your mistakes rather than being defeated by them. It doesn't benefit you to get discouraged. Stay busy and work hard. Think of your wake-up alarm clock as an *opportunity clock* and be positive, hopeful and confident about each day. Believe you can achieve your dreams and that nothing is impossible. Optimism improves your self-esteem, overall sense of well-being, and relationships with others. Being optimistic and hardworking are very important. A positive attitude and strong work ethic gives you confidence and makes you a winner. Hard work eliminates fear. A well-known motivational speaker once said: *F-E-A-R has two meanings: "Forget everything and run, OR, face everything and rise."* (Zig Ziegler). Being optimistic provides you with a positive focus to get back up and rise to any failure that knocks on your door.

❖ **Establish goals**

A goal is something that you want to accomplish. Goals will give you direction and allow your mind to focus. By setting goals for yourself, you are able to measure your progress because you have a fixed target in your mind.

It is difficult to achieve your dreams without charting a new course (goals) to get there.

If you don't know where you are going, you will have no way of charting a course, nor will you know when you have arrived. When you set goals, have confidence and commit 100% effort; with that commitment, you will become successful. Goals can be academic: my goal this year is to turn my D in Mathematics class to a C+. Or you may have a personal goal: I am going to improve my behavior and be more respectful to others. The first step in setting goals is to make them meaningful by writing them down. The next step is to prepare an action plan to accomplish your goals. Finally, you need to create a timeline to complete your goals.

Plan to win, prepare to win, and expect to win!

Start with small goals. Don't shoot for the moon right away. Slow and steady wins the race. Make your goals specific. The goal "I will change my behavior" is great, but it's so huge you probably won't have any idea how to start. Instead, set a smaller specific goal, like "I will stop being late to school."

Be positive. Make your goals something you're working toward, not trying to avoid. For example: "Stop eating junk food" is an unhelpful goal. It can cause feelings of shame or guilt. "Eat 3 servings of fruit and vegetables each day" is specific and positive.

Control your goals. Set goals that depend on what you can control because you cannot control others. If you set goals that require a certain response from others, you may end up feeling down if things don't go as you hoped. Remember, you are the only one who can control your performance.

Set goals that are specific. Having goals that are too big can make it difficult to establish a plan of action to achieve the goal. "I will be successful" is not specific. Success is different for everyone. Being successful can change on a daily or hourly basis. "I will graduate from high school," or "I will go to college and graduate with a degree in nursing" is more specific.

Make sure you can measure your goals. You should be able to tell when a goal has been achieved. Make sure you can tell whether you're "there" or "not." You will know that you have reached your goal of graduating from high school when you walk across the stage and receive your diploma in your hand.

Goals should be achievable. A goal that may not be achievable would be to become the smartest, richest or most powerful person in the world. A more achievable goal may be to receive a college degree.

Set a time limit for your goals. Effective goals should include a time plan as well as an action plan; otherwise, you could always be working towards a goal and never really get there. If you want to change your grade in mathematics from a D to a C+, make a plan and a time period. Work towards making it happen instead of thinking that it might happen "someday." Saying you'll get going "tomorrow" is the same as never starting at all. Tomorrow is a day that never comes. In order to change, you must not make excuses; you will achieve nothing by putting it off.

PLAN TO WIN!
PREPARE TO WIN!
EXPECT TO WIN!

When you plan your goals, you will have a roadmap of where you want to go and motivation to get there. Keep in mind that there will probably be roadblocks on your journey. If you run into a wall, find a way to climb it, go through it or work around it. Roadblocks should not stop you; change directions, DO NOT change the goal. The more you fall down and get back up, the closer you are to accomplishing your goals.

Chart a New Course! Establish Goals! Re-invent yourself!
Take the stairs instead of the elevator and be creative.
You can do it!

❖ **Learn how to problem solve skillfully.**

Without doubt, you are going to face problems at school, at home and in life. Use your problems and your ability to solve them as a learning experience. Identify and understand the problem. Be creative and find more than one solution. Have faith in yourself. Do not be negative and dwell on your problems. Remember that being negative can interfere with your ability to deal with solving a problem. Have faith in yourself and your ability to deal with your problems in a constructive way. Change the problem and negativity into something positive, which may help you more effectively deal with the situation. Give yourself a chance to focus on what is positive in your life. This may show you that you can deal with any challenge that may come your way.

The key is to learn to take control of your problem before the problem takes control of you!

"I'm dealing with my problems in a constructive way. It's going to take a while to solve them, but I'm on the right path." If you are seriously trying to deal with problems, chances are that you'll have some setbacks. Say good-bye to the setbacks, take necessary action, and then keep moving forward. Sometimes problems take a little longer to solve than you anticipated. Keep moving towards your goals, which will help you deal with the problem in a constructive manner. For example, if you continue to get bad grades, keep trying. Any progress on your grades is good progress. Let go of the past. Focus on moving forward, not on trying to go back. Let go of your mistakes. Instead of hating yourself for them, learn from them. Mistakes don't define you. Get as much information as you can. The more you know about the situation you're in and the options you have available to you, the better able you will be to deal with whatever the problem is.

Do a little Googling, talk to people who have dealt with problems like this before, and really think about what Plan B is instead of getting locked into Plan A. Stay calm. Don't panic or let yourself feel like the whole world is ending. So far, you've managed to get past every other problem in your life and the sun keeps rising; you must 100% believe that you are sure you can make it through this one too. Evaluate what resources you have. Everyone has resources available to them. Communicate, communicate, and communicate. You may find that talking more may be what's needed to fix the problem. There are few problems that cannot be solved or at least helped by talking with others. When you talk about your problems, you'll find that suddenly they become much easier to deal with.

Talk with the people attached to the problem that you're having. Talk to people who are experts. Talk to your friends and family. *Ask for help.* Just saying what you're struggling with is important and can cause someone to point out a good solution to help you solve a problem. Ask yourself what needs to happen to solve this problem. Once you've gotten as much information as you can and know what resources are available to you to make it happen, make a list of what needs to happen and when. You'll quickly see that you have all the skills you need to solve any problem, big or small. You have to be confident that everything will work out in the end. Now that you know what you need to do, do it!

❖ **Learn to think strategically.**

You definitely have thinking skills; the question is how well you think. If your thinking is not positive, your decisions may lead to bad decisions. Strategic thinking is a process that defines the manner in which you think. Thinking strategically is a way of looking at things and linking them together and is extremely effective. You can use strategic thinking to arrive at decisions that can be related to your school, work or your personal life. Strategic thinking isn't about thinking more or thinking harder; it's about thinking *better*. _Learn to "think outside of the box!"_

Thinking outside the box means to *"think differently* and be creative" instead of sticking to the same old ways. Keep an open mind! Avoid saying things to yourself that will shut down creativity rather than encourage it. Catch yourself anytime you say: "That won't work," "I haven't done it that way before," "I can't solve this problem," or "I don't have enough time." The thing that will hold you back from thinking outside the box more than anything else is negative thinking.

Thinking better and thinking strategically can be improved with the following action steps: _Keep an open mind._ A closed mind will not allow new ideas to enter and this is an important first step to thinking strategically. _Read and read and read._ Reading leads to imagination, increased concentration, and improved critical thinking skills. _Set clear goals._ Remember, start with small goals and build on success. _Have a sense of humor._ The ability to laugh at yourself and see the sense of humor in mistakes will make falling down and getting back up easier. _Don't believe everything you see or hear._ Play detective and discover the truth. Sometimes a big box with pretty wrapping does not tell you what is inside. Open it up and look inside! _Replace negative thoughts with positive thoughts._ "I can't do anything right," "I'm just not as smart as everyone else," and "school is a waste of time" are negative thoughts that represent low self-image. In order to think better, you need to have a self-image that is positive and strong. Stop yourself and say: "I can, and I will! I am a champion!"

❖ **Develop a strong positive network.**

Choose your network of friends wisely. Rather than hanging with the crowd that always lands in detention, find friends who keep up with their grades and participate in appropriate after-school activities. Look for classmates who share your interests and spend time with them. Stay clear of bad behavior and negativity so that it will not rub off on you. Good friends help you achieve your goals and support you through tough times. Spend less time with friends that bring you down. *Be aware of the "dream stealers."*

Dream stealers are liars who tell you that you don't have what it takes to be a winner. Their game plan is to make themselves look like winners at your expense. You don't need to play their game. A strong positive network consists of friends that accept you for who you are. There will always be someone who judges you for something. Don't let that attitude bother you. Remember that the only person you need to please is you. Learn from peers who are trying to re-invent themselves and are striving to be the best.

❖ **Embrace change.**

Why do you want to change and how will you change? Start with being positive: "I am a good person," "I am a hard worker," and "I have goals, but my behavior is not great and I want to improve my grades so that I can play football." If you feel like you need a change to whom you are it is definitely possible. Changing what you do can lead to a change in your self-esteem and help you re-invent yourself. Change is difficult and uncomfortable, but if you are determined to set and stick with a plan to change, it will happen over and over. The hardest part of change is knowing why you want to change.

Once you know why, continue to be positive: "I can and I will become the person I want to be," and "I will prove to myself that I can improve." Make sure it's what **you** want and not what others think you should want. If you don't actually embrace change, it won't come. Be patient. If change could come overnight, it wouldn't be worth it. You may not see results as soon as you had planned. It's also sometimes difficult to see change or results in yourself as quickly or easily as someone may be able to from the outside. You change a little every day, and it might be difficult for you to notice or monitor your own change, but it is happening. The next time you are faced with change, embrace new possibilities and step into new opportunities. Don't let the fear of change hold you back.

❖ **Fall down but never stay down.**

Life will knock you down. Instead of allowing your failures to paralyze you and slow you down, ask yourself: what can I do to learn from this, what can I do differently next time? Use your mistakes and failures as opportunities to keep moving towards your goals. Strategically think of the way you look at your definitions of success and failure. It's baby steps that make getting back up possible. Baby steps will help you reach your goals and allow you to focus on the things you have done well and will create positive encouragement to keep going. Remember the process of getting back up: one knee, and the second knee, and then you get up on one leg at a time and eventually you are standing tall.

When you fall down, don't see failure as a measure of who you are. You are not dumb because you failed one, two or three exams. You are not weak because you missed the winning basketball shot. Use these experiences to push forward rather than giving up. Believe that you are resilient and can bounce back from failure. Always, always look at failure as temporary. When something is temporary, that means that it will change because it is not permanent. If we did not fall down, we would have no reason to get back up. But this is not reality. Every one falls down. But it is about what you learn from mistakes and failures that is important and what makes you successful. You will actually be stronger and more resilient from falling down.

Remember, however, that failures aren't failures; they're opportunities. You can learn valuable lessons from falling down, and you may learn that falling down will improve being the best that you can be. Fall down early and fall down often, use your failures as fuel to get back up and keep going. Remember, each failure is a chance to grow stronger and wiser. You are resilient!

Getting knocked down, at times, may be beyond your control. You may not be responsible, but you are responsible for getting back up. ALWAYS!!

Chapter 13
RESILIENCY, ENDURANCE, TRIUMPH
#NeverGiveUp

If You Fall Down, Get Back Up. Work Hard. Reap the Rewards. Consider the following examples of Resiliency, Endurance and Triumph:

- Beyonce says she was a really shy, quiet student in school. She admits that as a child, she failed to win many singing and dancing competitions, and her early songs were just not good. Today she is a successful singer, songwriter, dancer, actress, and record producer. Throughout her career, she has sold an estimated 100 million records as a solo artist and has won 22 Grammy Awards. *(#nevergiveup)*

- Michael Jordan: "I've missed more than 9000 shots in my career. I've lost almost 300 games. Twenty-six times I've been trusted to take the game winning shot and missed. I've failed over and over again in my life. And that is why I succeed." *(#nevergiveup)*

- Wilma Randolph was the twentieth of twenty-two children. She was born prematurely and wasn't expected to survive. When she was four years old, Wilma contracted double pneumonia and scarlet fever which left her with a paralyzed left leg. At age nine, she removed the metal leg brace and began to walk without it. By thirteen, she developed a rhythmic walk which doctors claimed as a miracle. That same year, she decided to become a runner. She entered a race and came in last. For the next few years, every race she entered, she came in last. Everyone told her to quit, but Wilma kept on running. One day, she actually won. From then on, she won every race entered. Eventually this little girl, who was told that she would never walk again, went on to win three Olympic gold medals. *(#nevergiveup)*

- One of the most beautiful speaking voices on stage and screen belongs to James Earl Jones. Jones battled a severe stuttering problem from age nine until his mid-teens. During this time, the only way he could communicate with his teachers and classmates was by hand-written notes. *(#never give up)*

- It was not until he reached his fifties that Morgan Freeman became a movie star. *(#never give up)*

Winners Never Quit and Quitters Never Win
The Winner is always part of the answer.
The Loser is always part of the problem.
The Winner always has a program.
The Loser always has an excuse.
The Winner says "Let me do it for you."
The Loser says "That's not my job."
The Winner sees an answer for every problem.
The Loser sees a problem for every answer.
The Winner sees a green near every sand trap.
The Loser sees two or three sand traps near every green.
The Winner says "It may be difficult but it's possible."
The Loser says "It might be possible, but it's too difficult."
BE A WINNER.
-Vince Lombardi

Chapter 14
DR. C'S KEYS TO SUCCESS
#reinventyourself#plantowin
#preparetowin#expecttowin

Key #1: Start Small

This chapter will provide an opportunity for you to reinvent yourself and create a plan to become an awesome champion. I have shared events in my life that you can use to insert into your daily activities. Now it is time for you to put what you have read into practice. Success belongs to "you" if you are willing to work hard. "*Dr. C's Keys to Success*" will outline essential tools (keys) needed to open doors and gain motivation, desire, determination and commitment.

My keys to success will include soft skills and hard skills. Soft skills are talents that people increasingly take notice of. These skills are beneficial and are important to success. They are viewed as personal characteristics that enable someone to interact effectively and meaningfully with other people. Everyone looks at them – employers, employees, principals, teachers, and friends – everyone. Hard skills are abilities that are needed to show proficiencies in a given situation. For example, if you need to present information in an organized format, you will more likely need to be skilled in computer software applications to present data with spreadsheets. Other hard skills include typing, writing, mathematics, reading and specific teachable subjects you learn in the classroom. While soft skills and hard skills are equally important, most of Dr. C's Keys will focus on soft skills.

Soft skills are interpersonal (people) skills. An employer who is looking for employees with soft skills, might look for workers with soft skills which include getting along with others, good etiquette, patience, the willingness to listen, the ability to engage in small talk, to name a few. Some of these skills are simply not easily taught in the classroom, but they are key to building relationships and working together as a team. Soft skills don't just apply to the work place. They are important in all aspects of life where there is interaction between people. Additional skills that are necessary when we want to be successful and move ahead include adaptability, problem-solving, close observation, the ability to resolve conflicts, and teamwork. Basically, it boils down to just getting along with others. Your soft skills allow you to get the job done!

Many view soft skills as simply "behaviors." You know — the behaviors that your mother talked to you about and the types of behaviors reinforced in you as a child in school every day. These soft skills represent those personal qualities, those habits, those attitudes, those social competences, those graces that make a person a good person, a good employee or a great teammate or someone you like to be around … You know, those people you know who just fit. When we talk about a good fit, we can always recall a teammate or an acquaintance that we always want to be around: They light up the room with good energy. Everybody likes that person. Well, what makes that person so special is that they've learned those soft skills, those social graces, the ability to work and talk to people a certain way—those habits.

They're friendly and always optimistic. What do I mean by optimistic? They see the glass half full instead of half empty. Optimistic people are not always bellyaching and complaining about could haves, would haves and should haves. Who are some people with these great soft skills that you would want to be like? Your school leaders, teachers, parents, church leaders — all those people who just light up the room whenever they walk around. And if you watch those adults, you'll be able to see that they have those skills that allow them to grow and become more prosperous. So as we talk about Dr. C's Keys, I will talk to you about those soft skills that I have used to grow and have allowed me to be whom I am today.

The most important soft skill that I want to talk to you about is *"**STARTING SMALL.**"* As you read in my stories, I explained how I started small. In the first grade, I made an F+. My F+ turned into a D, and the D turned into a D+, and eventually a C- and a C+. I just continued to grow in my academia and became successful. But that was because I started small. I didn't set big goals like I was going to become a straight A student overnight, but I wanted to grow over time, so I set smaller goals. I understood that you had to embrace the small stuff. You know, you have to embrace the little things in life and stop looking at those big moments. Stop going for the grand slam or slam dunk when you can't even make a layup. Instead, start small and when you have consistent successes under your belt, big opportunities will come.

But you must first embrace the small things. For example, some are simple gestures, little things, like introducing yourself to a group or introducing a person to another person. When you are with someone, do you say, "Hi, my name is --. How are you?" Do you introduce yourself in such a way that people will want to introduce themselves back to you? Can you introduce a friend to another friend or introduce two people to each other? Can you give someone a bit of encouragement to keep working at something? How often do you encourage someone who is discouraged because of a past failure, because they didn't meet a goal or because they may have not just been able to do well in some endeavor? How often do you run up to that person and encourage them to keep trying? How often do you give someone a challenge to reach a little further? Do you allow your friends to just become complacent with low expectations or do you tell that person to go further? *"**Strive for 5"*** is how I like to say it and *"**Reach for the stars."*** These words won't necessarily change the world but encouragement of this type can initially help build success over time. Great and successful people who have many accomplishments will always tell you that they started small. When you start small, you discover that there are so many opportunities. I would like to challenge all of you to implement the first key to success as you "strive for 5", and "reach for the stars": <u>start small, take baby steps and do your best</u>.

An essential part of starting small is to be motivated and dedicated to success. Always do your best work to get started at your current level. Remember when I earned an F+? That was my best work at the time, but I needed to grow and develop a very strong work ethic. If there is one key that I want you to understand, it is that you have to start small and grow from where you are. You have to grow and if you start small and work extremely hard, you will do great things in life because you will get better over time. When you start small and you give your best work, you are developing a strong work ethic but you are also learning to be responsible in addition to learning to be accountable. That's a significant goal. You want be responsible and always, when looking back at your work, you want to ask, "Am I giving my 5-star effort?" Given my 5-star effort, "Am I doing all that needs to be done as I strive for 5?"

Remember, above all, the first skill that I want you to master is to start small, work really hard at starting small, never give up, grow small successes, turn failures into opportunities and always, always, always continue to Strive for 5.

Key #2: Set Goals

Writing down my goals allowed me to be all that I was supposed to be. Most people that I've met in my life go through life without bothering to set their own goals. Some don't even have them. Very few people whom I have met have specific measurable goals and even fewer have written these goals down. When I found myself walking through school watching the students with straight A's, I realized that the students who were doing really well in school, even the best athletes in the building, all had specific goals. They had goals written down. I didn't do that at first. I always wondered why you would write down something that you can't see. Then it occurred to me that when you write down your goals, you are developing a vision, and a vision allows you to become focused. I started writing down my goals and I started comparing myself to my friends. One of the distinguishing facts that I noticed between my friends and myself was that I had written down my goals in such a way that they provided me a road map to where I wanted to go. Consequently, I've discovered after 25 years working in education, I have accomplished every goal that I wrote down.

The first goal that I had written down was to *make the basketball team* at Thomas Dale High School. I was a junior and I had never played organized basketball a day in my life. I wrote the goal down and started developing a pathway to meeting that goal. And that meant I had to behave a certain way in school. That's a "soft skill." I had to be respectful in school; I had to get a job and be respectful in the work place; I needed to develop a network of support. That was the roadmap of success that was paved because I had written down my goals. And then when I compared myself to my friends who had not written down their goals, I discovered that they were dropping out of high school. They were not only dropping out of school but getting in all sorts of trouble. It was then I began to see that the difference was "focus".

You see, when you write down your goals, you actually become more focused on where it is you're trying to go. Remember that when you start small and you write down your goals, what it begins to do is raise your self- esteem. When I did that, I had the courage to stand up for myself, I had the courage to do the unpopular thing, I had the courage to step away from people who said they were my friends but they didn't really care about what I wanted to accomplish. I had the courage to get a job, and courage to be respectable in school. I had the courage to freely contribute my ideas and to stand up in class and try to answer a question even though they laughed at me at first. But because I was focused and I was starting small and I had written down my goals, my self- esteem started to increase.

When that happened, I started feeling more confident and my confidence in myself began to shoot through the roof. I started to believe in myself and do all the things that I needed to do to accomplish my goals. My goals provided a GPS. You know the GPS helps you navigate and give you directions to a location. In other words, it gives you a map. Well, goals do the same thing. Goals actually become your GPS. And you just drive until you reach your destination. The possibility that you will find the correct way your first time is very unlikely. I had to learn that. There are a lot of bumps and bruises along the way as you are trying to accomplish your goal. But what it does allow you to do is go forward with certain boldness and a belief in yourself that you will accomplish your goals no matter what. Your goals allow you to lead and you will eventually get there.

When you write down your goals, you have to first figure out what you want. Figure it out. What is it that you want? What things would you like to accomplish this year, in three years or the next five years? Write them down. Put them on a piece of paper and write down answers to your questions. I wanted to make the basketball team, then I wanted to be the star of the basketball team, and then I wanted to use basketball as a vehicle to go to college. After I got into college, I wanted to use my junior college to continue my education to go to a four-year college. Always make sure you write down *specific* goals and always try to put deadlines in your written goals. That means that you want to accomplish something within a certain period of time. That's why your goals should actually be realistic. After writing down my goals, I had to learn to write two or three action steps on how I planned to achieve the goal.

I knew, for example, that in order for me to make the basketball team, I needed to first impress the coach. Well, how was I going to impress the coach? I needed to go to class on time (Step 1); I needed to be eligible to play by making good grades (Step 2); I didn't need to have any disciplinary problems (Step 3). Those were my three action steps. You will need to do the same thing as well. As you write down your goals, make sure they are specific. Always put a deadline behind your goals and, for each goal, write two or three steps that you plan to take to reach your goal. And with that being said, your goal becomes your GPS - your navigational tool to reaching your plan.

Key #3: *Change Destructive Behavior*

I am constantly challenged with being mindful about things that can slow my growth, sort of like eating bad food. What do you do when you are doing things that are self-destructive and you know it is not good but you continue? We all have those problems, but how do you change those destructive habits that keep you from doing the things that are not good? That's an issue that we all have to deal with and it is also a great question. I want to talk with you about that and about how I was able to change my self-destructive behaviors - behaviors that worked against me and against my becoming Dr. C. Self-destructive behaviors are just behaviors that just rear their destructive heads, time and time again, not on a regular basis but just pop up from time to time. You've probably been doing them over and over, slowly over time. For example, back talking or interrupting people while they are talking and not saying "Excuse me." Can you change destructive behaviors? Sure, you can. I absolutely believe that you can do so because I was able to change.

One destructive behavior that I had was back in the early days when I was a teenager. During that time, we were all experimenting with cigarettes. And here I am trying to play basketball but everyone wants to smoke a cigarette afterwards. Now that was a destructive behavior. I had to change. When you had a goal such as mine, smoking cigarettes could be a detriment. Smoking affects one's ability to function as an athlete. Specifically, the effect of smoking cigarettes on athletes can be described very simply: it reduces their endurance and it impacts on their performance. Also, your muscles need oxygen to perform their function and athletes who smoke get tired more quickly and won't be able to build muscle as effectively.

I had to change that habit of smoking cigarettes with my friends and get focused on getting endurance to run the entire four quarters of the game. If you want to be "top in your field," avoiding anything that is destructive to your performance is essential. And trust me, I was no superman. I was no great leaper, no great jumper or a great athlete, but I was a hard worker and I had to become disciplined and a model of self-mastery to the outside. But you have to understand that I always felt that I was undisciplined and a procrastinator and I lacked self-control. I soon realized that in order for me to make some changes, I had to follow some key steps in my life.

First, I had to feel the pain: You have to have a setback. The setback that I had was when I got cut from the basketball team in the tenth grade. I just wasn't ready and being cut from the team made me feel a whole lot of pain. I mean, when you get cut and you know you are the best person on the team, and something you dream about having is not going to happen — you know what I'm talking about…. you feel a whole lot of pain and that pain motivated me to make a change in my life. Sometimes you need to be in a painful place that you need to get out of. When you are in that painful place, allow yourself to see and feel the pain and ask yourself whether it's time for you to change. If you keep getting in trouble in school, is it time for you to change? If you keep getting written up and suspended, is it time for you to change? If you can't make the football team, is it time for you to change? If you are making straight F's and you are not going to graduate on time, is it time to change? What do you want to do about it? You need to get out of that painful place.

The second thing I had to do was turn inward. I had to look inside myself and face my problem. Turn around and look at it. Admit that I have a problem and it's my problem. You just have to turn around and look at the big elephant in the room that's causing you not to live the way you want to live. And one of the biggest excuses in making these changes is that we avoid them, and refrain from thinking about them: 'I don't want to talk about it.' But you know what happened to me, my problems got worse and worse. I just went downhill and I started learning to distract myself by looking for other things to keep me busy instead of facing the problem in front of me; I started to blame other people for my problem. For example, you might blame other people for why you get suspended from school instead of looking at yourself and your own behaviors. You need to realize you're in a painful cycle and that scary cycle only leads downward. So you have to acknowledge it.

The next thing is to accept your situation the way it is right now and once you accept it, you begin to understand that you can actually make a change. But you must first feel it and acknowledge it. You must pick one thing about that problem that you can change, like apologize. Apologize to the teacher for being disruptive in her classroom and promise not to do it again. That's it. That's a small, distinct thing that you can change immediately. And then you work on it. You stay with your promise. I told you I was not going to be disruptive in your class and I'm not! No matter what distractions come my way, I am not going to be disruptive in your class. And once you promise not to be disruptive, learn to come to class on time and commit to being prepared. Commit to it. Come to class every day. Remember whatever change you decide to make, commit to it. Remember that. Start small and then commit to it. When you commit to it, you're standing up publicly. You are saying, "I'm committed to making a change." People will begin to look up to you and say: "WOW, Look at the change! It's remarkable!"

Finally, I had to learn that I must be committed to the change. You have to learn to BELIEVE that you can change. You see in the beginning, you're always going to have doubts: Can I do this job? Can I come to class prepared? Can I study every night? You're going to be talking negatively to yourself all the time. Those are going to be the obstacles that are going to come your way. But every time you mess up, there will be this amazing opportunity for you to get better. I've always said that, "Every time I messed up, there was an opportunity for me to improve." Every failure is an opportunity for success. And that is why you have to not believe in negative self-talk. And that is all it is: simply 'negative self-talk' that comes your way.

It's just a tape that is played in your head over and over again, but through discipline, you can tell your brain you can do this, and when your brain says you can't do this, you have to actually override that signal and say, "I've seen other people do this and if other people can do this then so can I, if I try. I want to say that again: "When your brain tells you that you can't actually do this, I want you to look in the mirror and say "If other people can do this, so can I." Say it over and over, "If other people can do this, so can I and I only have to try." And then you find support. There is a lot of support around you everywhere you go. I want you to remember that part of my change, eliminating destructive habits, meant that *I had to actually change my destructive environment.* Remember the part about the desk when the teacher told me that I needed to have a desk, a place to study in my house, I went out and bought a desk, a lamp and watch. What I was doing was creating the right environment to change my destructive habits. So, you'll have to do the same thing.

There were times when I had to stay after school to create the right environment to study. You will have to create a place where you can set up an environment that works for you. I was not a failure, but a big success and I was able to learn. It is to your advantage to try to avoid and change those destructive environments every day, just as I did.

Key #4: Surround Yourself with Successful People

One of the areas that I needed to improve as I charted a new course in my life was to separate myself from negative influences, and I needed to be around people who wanted the same things that I wanted. Well, how do you get those things? If you really want to get to a new destination, you need to travel with different travelers. You can't say you want better and always be around people who want worse. Then you just have the crab in the bucket mentality and you end up not getting out of the bucket. I realized that I wasn't going to accomplish my goals in life if I continued to stay in my environment and that I needed to make different decisions in my life. It was then I understood what the term "mentor" meant, and I needed to get some new people in my life that could help me. There are so many valuable benefits of having a wonderful mentor. I love mentors. I would not be where I am today if it were not for mentors in my life. There are so many benefits not only for you, the one receiving the mentoring, but also benefits from the person providing the mentoring. For you, the mentee, the person being advised, you receive advice and encouragement that is constructive. If you have someone in your life that will help you and give you that unbiased opinion about what it is that they would like for you to know, then you have to learn to accept that constructive criticism.

I'll tell you a story: when I was playing basketball, I didn't understand how to play organized basketball. I was a street ball player and I played on the playground, but when I finally started playing on a team, I realized that everything was different, especially the rules. Importantly, I needed to understand the rules and the fundamentals of playing organized basketball. I had to play with friends that played organized basketball, learn how to play the game effectively and use my talent. I had to go out and get mentors, people who knew how to play: they understood rebounding; they understood boxing out; they understood running the ball; they understood running plays; they just understood those things. I needed experienced people in my life who would tell me when I was messing up. Now, often times you look at your coach, who is really your mentor, the one who you may or may not want to listen to, and sometimes they tell you something that actually hurts your feelings, but if you can listen to them, what they are actually telling you will actually help you accomplish your goal. But you must listen with a positive attitude and use what your mentors are saying to your advantage.

Attitude is everything. Your attitude actually determines your altitude. Mentoring allows you to receive that type of impartial advice and encouragement. Mentoring develops a supportive relationship. You actually have go-to people in your life. When you are in trouble, you can actually go to them and they will assist you with problem solving. I could also see improvement in my own self-confidence and they were always willing to teach me things about life and about what I was trying to do. They were there to encourage me as I reflected on my athletic performance. They were awesome. But what I also learned was that my group was also benefitting. They had an opportunity to *Pay It Forward*. They had the opportunity to reflect on their own life and share those highs and lows or pitfalls that they wanted me to avoid. It made them feel better about themselves – and it helped elevate me. I saw their satisfaction about themselves also improve. It allowed them to see me as someone they could show the way and clear the path. They also advocated for me. It is awesome having someone in your corner that will speak up for you. It gave me an opportunity to work on my interpersonal skills.

I remember one of my mentors was Coach Cham Pritchard. I told you about how he taught me to shake a hand with a firm grip and high five. He also taught me how to shake a hand like a man and look another man in the eye, eye to eye and introduce yourself properly. Those are the skills that allowed me to expand my relationships. So, when we talk about mentoring, remember that mentors can become lifelong mentors and they are ones that you can call on for the remainder of your life. They will follow your career and send you words of encouragement. You can <u>always</u> call them. Find and surround yourself with good people, people that provide counsel, people that you respect and people that you strive to emulate. This key is extremely important.

Key #5: Dream Big!

I have always been a dreamer. I have always found the opportunity to look up at the sky and just visualize and just dream. I have always been a dreamer. I've always imagined myself in different places doing other things. I would always read comic books and imagined myself being the super hero. I would always dream big and I want <u>you</u> to always dream big. Since as long as I could remember, I would always have these crazy fantasies and visions of doing and achieving super things in my life. But I'm sure all of you have done the same.

We are all dreamers and I know I am not the only dreamer out there. What I have learned is that society, your friends or your peer group might work to dismiss some of your dreams as just pure nonsense. They will say, "Man, stop dreaming, stop dreaming." But there are enormous benefits to dreaming big. You have to learn to dream. If you are a crazy dreamer like me, then you and I are from the same place. Dreaming involves holding on to a tight vision for a better life. I wanted a better life. I no longer wanted to live in the circumstances I was living in, so I would always dream and have a vision of a better life, one where success was abundant. In a better life in which I was extremely successful, I had children that were going to college and I was living in a life of abundance. I did not want to worry when I turned the light switch on, if the light was going to come on; if I went to start my car, I wasn't worried if the car would start or not.

I know that while getting there might be difficult, accomplishing your dream can be laden with a lot of rocks. As you travel, you're going to have setbacks and failures along the way, but I'm here to tell you it is really worth it. It is worth it! Anyone who achieves their goals knows the cost of what they had to put up with in order to get there. Yet we occasionally stop dreaming.

Circumstances can allow us to snuff out our dream or we get so caught up within our current circumstances, we forget to hold tight to those dreams. But I'm here to tell you that holding tight to your dreams gives you the assurance that you can do *anything*. And you can and will do anything to accomplish your dream and make them a reality. So, the truth of the matter is you must never give up on your dream. Never give up on your dream. Don't ever throw in the towel on what it is you want to accomplish when the going gets tough. Don't give up but learn persistence! You have to go through the storm, and you have to endure the pain that will allow you to avoid another failure. Keep your head in the sky and focus on not giving up. Dreaming often becomes a reality because you have built a platform for growth and success.

It all starts with a big dream. You have to understand that there are plenty of benefits to just being normal. I get it, but what you don't want is to become complacent and compliant and subdued. There is nothing quite like being a dreamer because it is exciting, and it's thrilling when you have wild visions of doing extraordinary things. You are boldly entering a future of hope and endless possibilities.

How do you dream big? When you go to a kindergarten class or watch a little baby, you eventually see them begin to dream big. It's part of who we are and it is part of our genetic makeup. See, you are made to dream. Even babies when they are small are not hindered by a standard – they are not hindered by anything holding them back, so you are made to dream. When you are young, you might say, "I want to play in the NFL" but when you become a senior, it's like, "I want to graduate." Well, that's what happens when you just dismiss your dreams as being silly or unrealistic. But who is to say your dreams are silly or unrealistic? Who's to say that your dreams can't be accomplished? Just because something goes against the grain or runs in the opposite direction of what people say is acceptable, it does not mean it is impossible. So we can all use a bit of childlike amusement. There is absolutely nothing wrong with it and if your dreams don't scare you, then they're not big enough.

When I first started dreaming of becoming Superintendent of Schools, I thought: "Wow, there is no way in the world I could run an entire school division when I am struggling to just graduate from high school." So, it scared me. I was actually afraid that this dream was entirely too big. But what I learned when I looked at my mentors was that the only thing that was holding me back from achieving that dream was me. I had to learn to get out of my own way because I was becoming my own worst enemy. In so many of my failures, it was because of me and it was because I didn't believe wholeheartedly in myself.

First, what I want you to do is THINK. What you actually think is what you become. So, we dreamers are special people. We have a unique way of looking at things deeply enough to see them right before our very eyes. And that holds some serious power. Why? Because thoughts are actually things. What we think, we actually become. Many of you have heard that expression before, but here it is very powerful. There have been many persons in history that achieved incredible results and were able to deeply envision their dreams before they became a reality. Look at your super stars. They'll tell you the same thing. I have learned that every single person who has gone on to do something sensational in life will tell you this: that their accomplishments started as dreams.

When you dream it, you become it. When you go and check out cars, why do you think you should test drive that car before you actually buy it? Well, you know test driving is a powerful selling feature. Sales people know that if they can sit you in the car, you will begin to dream of actually owning it. If you hold that new pair of sneakers in your hand, or when you go to the shoe store and you see the new Jordan's and the salesperson tells you to put them on, they know the act of physically putting on those shoes or driving the car gives you the feeling of what it's like to having it. You begin to dream of owning it and then that dream becomes a reality. You know what I mean.

I really want you to understand that thoughts are things. They are things! No words are truer. As a dreamer, dream big and see your dreams as vividly as the light of day. If you are a dreamer, DREAM BIG! Then, I want you to write them down. Remember, that was Key #2 – WRITE THEM DOWN AS CLEARLY AS YOU POSSIBLY CAN. Don't allow other people to say, "Boy, that's just crazy" or "Girl, that doesn't make any sense" just because your dreams are big. They should be huge! Remember, they should be huge. That's when you know you have hold of something worthwhile.

When you begin to dream, your focus or vision actually changes because you begin to see and understand things differently. For example, two of you may go out to the same place to the same party. You might witness two friends arguing in a corner. One person might say that the party was awful because all he saw were people arguing. Your friend might say, "I didn't want to be here because all we see are people fighting. Another person goes to same party, laughs, dances, and meets new people. He goes home and tells everyone, "Yeah, I had one of the best times in my life." What separates these two perceptions? **FOCUS!** How can one person see people getting along and another person see people bickering? How can one person go home thinking he had a great time, while the other person says everyone was fighting. **It's focus!** Focus is everything. Later, we will talk about it as a Key. What you focus on, you get more of.

Now, as you begin to dream, you start to see things differently, and guess what happens? Your life begins to move. You begin to move in a particular direction and that means your subconscious mind, thoughts in back of your mind, move you to think differently. Your brain is a super, super, super computer and when you begin to dream your brain begins to create a pathway for you accomplishing your dream. Isn't that powerful? Your mind begins to develop a pathway and you begin to move in that direction and that is why dreams are so important. You begin to realize areas in your life that you need to improve and self-improvement becomes a necessity. During my years in grade school, for example, I began to focus and see my life moving in a different direction. I began to understand I needed to improve my grades. You see, I started realizing then, but fully understand now, that self-improvement is a necessity. It was not an option. One might think: I can make D's and get away with it. No, that is not an option: I had to make C's and B's; I had to become eligible to play basketball and I had to become eligible to play at college level. As a result of my level of thinking, I knew I had to meet those college entrance level requirements.

I began to understand that I needed to stay after school and attend the writing workshops, the math workshops. I asked for extra credit. Self-improvement became a necessity and not just an option. When I failed and didn't pass the test, what I learned was *resiliency.* I recovered so much and I bounced back up because I knew how to respond to the pain. But I also learned to effectively manage my time.

Your time management is going to grow mentally because you are going to use your mind wisely. And then, again, you don't believe failure is an option. It doesn't make sense to you anymore. What you want is within your reach because you have dreamed it. You will learn to seek inspiration in others – those mentors -- and they're going to become the people that you emulate (copy). They're going to become inspirational for you right along the way. And when those bad habits come back, you are not going to pay any attention to them. You are going to start sweating the small stuff, those small changes that you need to make because you realize that as a dreamer, the little things add up. Remember the hustle points I told you about? They didn't seem like much in the moment, but over time they amounted to a lot. They helped push us forward. A few minutes wasted or gained here or there becomes important over time.

I began to understand that if I didn't want to continue to see free lunch, I needed a new route. I didn't like receiving free lunch and I wanted to work my way around what was typical. I wanted to work and pay my own way, so when I got a job bagging groceries, I began paying my own way and I knew it would teach management responsibilities. As I charted my own course in my life, I began to look at my budget and do some things differently; for example, I didn't buy sodas as often as I used to. Little by little, those small achievements began to stack up.

In the beginning, a specific dream seemed so far away, but little by little I saw myself actually accomplishing those dreams or moving towards them. I never thought about the huge amount that lay ahead of me, but little by little, I was getting the small wins: one achievement here, another achievement there and eventually, it all began to add up and those wins just started to stack up one by one until eventually I was graduating and ultimately setting my sights on becoming a Superintendent.

Key #6: **Build Your Stamina**

I want to talk with you quickly about endurance and sticking with your plan. Endurance refers to the power to last and to withstand hard work. Typically, in sportsmanship, and in life in general, it refers to training, exercising to increase your stamina, and increasing your ability to stay in the game. Endurance is a term used that is usually associated with your ability to not get tired and to sustain a high level of activity over a long period of time. Now, I learned a lot about endurance back when I was trying to play basketball and when I was trying to increase my grades in school. So, my first experience with endurance was that I first had to overcome destructive habits.

When I was in high school, it was cool to smoke cigarettes. Everybody had a cigarette back in those days. You actually had a smoking section in the high school. During class or in between class you could actually go out and have a cigarette. I was with my friends and we would pass that cigarette around. But I never liked it because what I found was it hampered my ability to play basketball: I couldn't run the entire floor, and I couldn't sustain a high level of performance throughout the four quarters of the game because I could not catch my breath at all. I LACKED ENDURANCE. I had to learn to get rid of those destructive habits and build my stamina. That meant I had to train a lot differently. It also meant my workout was critical in order to build endurance.

You need endurance in everything. In life, once you understand what endurance is and what endurance does for you, you'll be able to sustain a high level of performance throughout your entire life. I suggest to you that your FIRST STEP TO ENDURANCE IS PREPARATION. Preparation is absolutely vital for endurance training. What you need to do is learn to prepare yourself for what is about to happen. And it doesn't matter what your goal is. It doesn't matter if you are trying to make the basketball team. It doesn't matter if you are trying to pass a certain class.

It doesn't matter what you are training for. You must understand that there are some critical components that you need to pay attention to in order to optimize your performance; in other words, there are certain things that you need to do. I had to understand that there were certain things that I needed to do. For example, *I had to learn if I was going to be able to play* four quarters. I also had to learn proper hydration, what I needed to eat, and all the warm-ups that I needed to take into account. And then to top it off, I had to learn to get my rest and skip things that would keep me up all night. Preparation is extremely important to endurance.

The <u>SECOND STEP IS DISCIPLINE.</u> Once you prepare yourself, you need to know you have to stick to the plan. That is definitely essential if you plan to endure. You have preparation, and then you have to be disciplined and stick to the plan. This is endurance. What are some of the benefits of endurance and stamina? Health is one. Health is going to be a positive outcome from endurance training. Your mental ability is going to improve as well. What is more important, however, is your adaptability. You are going to learn how to change according to the goal. You are going to be flexible and adaptable no matter what the situation is. When we talk about building stamina, you need to always remember the story that I told you about my desk. That was building my endurance enough to stick with the process of improving my grades – I needed a safe place to work. I started small. You have to start small and slowly increase the intensity and eventually you'll start to change your ability to compete. Build your stamina!

Key #7: Five Ways to Overcome Failure

There is a Japanese proverb that says, "If you fall seven times, stand up eight." Well, what does it mean? To put it bluntly, failure hurts. I never failed and didn't cry. And sometimes the pain is so bad you don't know what you are going to do. It is actually a very painful experience and one that many of us work tirelessly to avoid. We spend our entire life trying to avoid failure. I want you to think about the numerous times you've spent trying to overcome failure. Often, failures' effects can be long lasting. Many of our failures leave a mark not only on our bodies but on your minds and it creates another mental hurdle that can be very difficult for you to overcome in later years. When I failed to make the basketball team in my tenth-grade year, it could have left a mental scar because it left me feeling ashamed of myself. That hurdle could have been, 'I am a mistake,' not 'I wasn't good enough to make the team or 'I didn't have the skills to make the team.' I could have easily said, 'I am not worthy to make the team,' and that is something different. Failure can leave you ashamed of yourself but not guilty that you didn't do enough to accomplish a goal. That's when I learned that *failure is necessary*. I needed those failures in order to become Dr. C.

When I failed, I tended to ponder and to search for a new meaning in my life. I wanted to explore the potential for possible answers and solutions for achieving my goal. In fact, I've learned that failure was a crucial part in me actually achieving my goal. It acted as a guiding light and it chiseled me to become the man I am today, so I have learned to embrace failure because it played such an important role in improving every action afterwards. Significantly, I was able to build off those failures throughout my life.

But everyone talks about how important failures are in life. It's hard to overcome failures to achieve your goals when you can see that what's in front of you equates to pain and agony. But you can overcome failures to achieve your goals even when all you can see is what's in front of you and that's pain, suffering and agony.

We've all experienced our share of failure. Some of my failures have been monumental. I know just how much it hurts to fail and to fail on a massive scale. Failures have made many marks on my life and it was not a simple matter of putting a Band-Aid on a bloody scar or holding a towel to my nose because it was bleeding. Sometimes failure leaves a lasting mark and the healing takes a lot of time. But through it all, I've come to some important realizations that I want to share that I have learned as I have pushed through my failures.

#1: NOTHING WORTHWHILE COMES EASY
Nothing worthwhile comes easy. We live in a dollar menu world – have it your way. We want things now and we don't want to wait for things. Why should we want to wait when we can just point and click and what you want shows up on your doorstep? Everything is based on high speed Internet – from the dollar menu to tweeting. It creates impatience and the belief that we don't have to wait for ANYTHING. It's not a wonder that failure actually hurts when we don't accomplish our goals. We are so used to getting what we want and getting it without having to work hard for it. But I need you to understand that it takes time to accomplish your goals. And during that time, you must make the journey towards overcoming your failures and building on your losses because that's how your failures actually build your character and YOU build new understandings. As you reach new understanding, you discover a deeper meaning to your life.

#2: IGNORE THE HATERS – THE NAYSAYERS
They will always be out. Remember: you're human and your mind and body work to avoid pain. In fact, it does just about

everything to avoid pain in any capacity. Part of the pain of failing has to do with dealing with other people who tell you, "I told you so." Have you ever had a friend tell you, "I told you so", or "Listen to me, you should quit while you are ahead?" I've had people tell me that a number of times. Well, we call them haters or naysayers. And they will always be around in full force, but don't listen to them. I need you to ignore their calls and their cries to celebrate your demise. They just want to be crabs in a bucket. What I want you to do is keep your head down and keep plugging away. Just realize that people will always be there to celebrate your demise. They will celebrate your failures. But the true friends will be there to celebrate your successes and inspire and push you to achieve your goals.

#3: SUCCESS ALWAYS LEAVES CLUES
Success always leaves clues, so you need to have an investigative personality and search for those clues. While failures might be difficult, there are also times when we tend to search for clues. Success also leaves clues. Do you get what I'm saying? Seek and you shall find. Search for someone who has been successful. Remember when I told you to search for those mentors? Search for them and look at their success and try to COPY what they've done. And copy how they've overcome failures. Notice how they've overcome those failures, and then look for clues: What did they do? How long did it take? How many times did they fail? When you look for examples of people who rose against failures, look at people like Michael Jordan who missed the shot more often than he hit the shot, but he never stopped taking the shot. People simply don't realize that some of the most successful people have failed the most times. But the most significant distinction is that those people never gave up! The biggest difference between those that succeed and those that don't is their unrelenting spirit of persistence.

I remember there were times when I was bullied in school. In fact, I was bullied in high school. And I would do everything to avoid the bullying. But what I learned was that trying to avoid the bullying just empowered the bully. One day, I was coming out of a grocery store and a bully saw me leaving. I immediately jumped on my bike and I was going to ride down the road and get away from him, but he yelled at me and said, "Man, get back here. I'm supposed to beat you up." I immediately stopped my bike, turned around and said, "Why is it that you hate me, that you want to fight me? We've had no beef, no squabble." And I stared at him. Now, he was a much bigger man; he was stronger, but I stared at him because I was tired of running. And then he looked at me and said. "Man, we good, we good." I then got on my bike and I rode away. See. Overcoming failure is also a chance to face your fears, a chance to overcome that innate desire to run away and hide in a corner. You have to stand up for it. When I did that I had an incredible feeling that I had what goes along with standing up. It was an invaluable feeling that paved the way for a lifetime of me achieving goals.

#5: USE YOUR FAILURE AS A LEARNING EXPERIENCE

I remember one time when I was at Liberty University and I was working on my Master's degree. At the end of the Master's degree, there is an End of Course exam. In my case, you had to pass the State's exam in order to graduate. I had spent hours and days and days of studying. I went into the exam extremely confident, almost over confident that I was going to ace this exam. I failed the exam! It was the week of and before graduation. I was devastated. It was an important test and I couldn't pass the exam. What I had to do was realize that I didn't read the questions and I didn't answer the questions because I just wanted to hear myself talk, so I just wrote a nice essay, but it was not related to the questions. Subsequently, I had to learn to read the test, make an outline, and then answer the questions. I learned from my mistakes. I had to acknowledge what I had failed to do. I was then able to push forward when I did that and was able to put it behind me. I had to ask myself why did I fail, where did I go wrong, what could I have done differently? Was it my plan, did I fail to see something I should have seen, did I read the test carefully, or did I just jump in and answer a question just because I thought I knew I was smart? Sometimes being over confident can be a bad habit. I had to really think about what had happened and I had to use that knowledge to improve myself and try again. Remember, as long as you don't give up, you can always overcome failure to achieve your goals.

Key #8: Strive for Progress, Not Perfection

This is your "Why." We always talk about the Why. Why is the motivator of your actions and basic beliefs? What you're trying to do is your Why? What motivates you? What is your passion? What makes you excited? What makes you happy? How do you have fun? What are your dreams? What are your goals? What is your definition of success?

I have learned that all of us have some sort of goal we are trying to reach. Many times, I had goals that I had not even fully formulated — a goal in my mind or a pathway. I've learned that if I had something to do, more than likely, I had to break an old habit. I wanted to be successful at work or at play, and I wanted to make good grades. Sometimes these goals can be a bit vague in their scope. Because I didn't have a pathway to achieving those goals, I was just left with the general sense of wanting to accomplish things in life, but I didn't have a desire to see those goals come to fruition. I had to learn that the things I wanted to accomplish were the things that I saw as defining me as successful. For me, that was the big picture.

Sometimes that big picture was so big I didn't understand what steps I needed to take to get me there. The goal can seem so overwhelming sometimes that you may feel you don't have the time or the resources or the awareness to see the steps you need to get yourself where you want to go. And when that happens, you start to make excuses: I started to say things like, "That goal wasn't really mine." If you find yourself expressing or thinking such a thought, it might be that you are concerned about something you couldn't do or you shouldn't do – it's not your Why. You don't start because you think you are going to fail. I actually thought I was going to fail. I didn't deserve to go to the University of Virginia. I didn't think I deserved to play basketball at Liberty University. It was simply because the goal seemed so big I thought I was going to fail. For me, often times, this was because I felt like I had unrealistic expectations. Many of us might feel that way – that if we are not perfect in our pursuits, we are a failure. I believed that if I didn't hit every free-throw, if I didn't slam-dunk the ball a certain way, if I wasn't electrifying the crowd, if I didn't make straight A's, or if I wasn't perfect in my pursuits, I was a failure. That was very, very concerning to me and those were the dead weights that were keeping me from progressing: I was focused on perfection and not progress.

I had to learn that I was human. We are all human and we are all imperfect. That is what actually made me a unique person and aware that I was awesome. I had to actually say those things: We're all human, we're all imperfect. It's what makes each of us unique. But guess what! Everyone is awesome! I had to stop eliminating the idea that perfection should be a goal because the outcome would always be failure. You see, when you focus on perfection, perfection becomes your goal. The outcome will always be failure. It does not mean that you don't set the bar high.

I had expectations of attending the University of Virginia and graduating with my doctorate. I had expectations of playing Division-1 basketball; I had expectations of being the first college graduate in my family. So absolutely, you should set the bar extremely high, but I had to learn to focus on progress, not perfection. I also had to focus on the process, on the now, not the outcome or on the steps that I needed to take along the path. *I began to focus on my journey, not my destination*: I wanted to play Division-1 basketball, but I knew I first needed to graduate from Richard Bland College. I strived for improvement. You need to first strive for improvement — learning, growing and understanding.

I had to strive for excellence and awesomeness, but still without imperfection. I always had to allow myself some wiggle room because I did not always accomplish the goal. And if I didn't make it to the school of my choice, I had to allow myself to make it to "A" school. Even though you may not make it to your place of choice, or school of choice, you have to allow yourself wiggle room.

If you give yourself some wiggle room, there is knowledge and comfort that even if you veer off the path just for a little bit, the path is still within your reach and you are still headed in the right direction. For example, even if you sidestep or get in trouble, you are aware that there was a time when you were trying to avoid getting in so much trouble. And last year, you may have gotten ten referrals for disciplinary issues. And this time you set a goal of not getting in as much trouble as last year. But something happened and you could not help getting a referral. You veered off the course. That's okay. You veered off course but now you know the path is right there in front of you and all you have to do is get back on the road. Get back on that pathway again and you'll be okay. See, that's knowledge and comfort that if you ever veer off the path just for a little bit, the path is still within your reach and you're still headed in the right direction.

Now, where do you start? I have learned that to make lasting change, change has to be meaningful. Change has to be meaningful to not anyone else but YOU. It can't be something that you feel is imposed on you, but you have to choose it. You can't do it because the principal wants you to do it, or the coach wants you to do it; you have to be a star because you have chosen to be a star. You have to choose it. It has to be something *you* value. I wanted to be the first person in my family to go to college and to graduate with my degree. So, it was my goal. It had to be valuable to me, and it had to be something I believed in. It had to be something I had to get behind and commit to do because I had to do all the work and I had to make sure the work was worth it. I had to ask myself, why do you want to make this change? And you have to be honest with yourself. It has to be something that is meaningful and that you can call on when you are struggling along your journey. It has to be something that will help keep you on the right path by putting one foot in front of the other to keep making progress when the going gets tough.

I started running in these mud races in which we had to run five miles over sixteen obstacles. It was cold day. Just bitter cold! It was also a rainy day and about forty-five degrees outside. On this particular day, we had to run 3 1/2 hours over 16 obstacles through water and mud, climb ropes – everything including traversing upside slippery mountains, everything we could possibly have to deal with that day. It had gotten to the point where I was cold, I was bleeding, and I was tired. I felt like I was just going to give up. I was literally at the point where I was ready to hold my hand up and ask for someone to come and pick me up. But why was I there? I wanted to work my way through those obstacles – I wanted to break through, so I kept putting one foot in front of the other even though I wasn't making a lot of progress, but I had to understand that my progress was very small because it was just one step in front of the other. Eventually, my second wind came back and my stride came back, and I started getting better and next thing you know, I was back running again.

But you have to break through and keep putting one foot in front of the other. You have to keep making progress even when the going gets tough. Once you know your "why" you have to write it down. You see, I understood that I wanted to be the first college graduate in my family. Why? Because both of my parents had dropped out of high school in the sixth grade. My father had served two tours in Vietnam, fought nobly for his country and he wanted me to have a much better day and a much better life than him and I wanted to stand on his shoulders and do much better. I had to write down my goals. Writing them down allowed me to have a picture of what I was trying to accomplish. You need to write them down because they get etched in your brain – your "why." And then you need to write down the reason or reasons you want to achieve your goal.

And you need to keep it somewhere where you can readily reference it to keep you on track. That's how you maintain your focus.

What can you do right now to help you reach your goal? It's good to know the big goal is there, but now you need to focus on the process, the pathway, in order to be ultimately successful. You want to focus on *each* step along the path that helps you reach your bigger goal. Don't focus on the outcome, just focus on the next step. I call that the "incremental growth" but you can call it *baby steps*. You can call it "making small changes," or you can call it "One step at a time." For example, you want to make better grades. There are all kinds of ways you can make better grades. To make better grades, you need to study, get your sleep, avoid negative friends, and stay after school to get additional help. As a big picture, when you look at all the possible options, the list can be endless, or it can be overwhelming. So, you need to hone it down even further. What I had to do if I was going to make the process more manageable was focus on just one step at a time, one small change that would help me achieve my goal over time.

I want you to remember that you are making progress.
Focus on progress, not perfection!
....and from the Carolina Panthers: "Keep pounding!"

Key #9: When You Fall, Get Back Up

"I've not failed; I've just found ten thousand ways that won't work." This statement is attributed to Thomas Edison. This is one of the key sayings in my life. I have not failed; I have just found ten thousand ways that won't work. I've had many more failures than successes in my life, and probably the success that stands out the most in my mind is becoming a superintendent, and the process of actually becoming a superintendent. I graduated in 2006 with my doctorate from the University of Virginia. I thought at the time that I had met all the prerequisites to becoming a superintendent. Every hurdle they told me I needed to satisfy, I had gone back and accomplished, and I had been told I had done a masterful job in doing so. But I didn't get called to be superintendent until 2016 when Halifax County, North Carolina, gave me an opportunity to become Superintendent of Schools. During the course of almost ten years, I had applied for the position of superintendent almost 18 times and I had 18 rejections. That can be disheartening to some, and it was for me at times. I just didn't understand why I would strike out so much. And when you first look at it, you might say, "I was not meant to be a superintendent. That is why no one is hiring me to become a superintendent." After 18 tries, some people would quit and just say: 'I will just remain where I am and retire.'

But I told you the story of the Tuskegee Airmen who continued to practice even though they were not allowed to fight as their country's pilots. So even though I had failed so many times and had so many rejection letters that I could wallpaper my wall and look at them every morning, I looked at them as a source of opportunity. This included every person who had been hired and *beat me out*. I studied their career. I studied and learned their ways. I began to eventually hone in on a huge set of skills that I was able to sharpen as well as hone in my practice and learn from the mistakes of others, so when I finally was called up to be

Superintendent in Halifax County, it was just an awesome experience because I was ready!

I went to a small school system with limited resources, but I had a vast tool box – I had a vast number of experiences after 18 tries. That counts! When they said they needed a finance person, I learned finance; someone who understood student services, I learned; when they wanted someone who understood reading instruction, I did that. How to build schools? I learned that. If you continue to look at your failures as obstacles, and then learn to overcome those obstacles, you're going to find a way that works. So as I continued to recall all those things, I remembered that it's not about the work and it's not about the failures; it's about how many times you can get knocked down and get back up. You see, it's not about the number of times you get knocked down but the number of times you get back up again. And that's what I want you to understand. Life is not about the number of times you fall down but the number of times you get back up after you fall. That's what makes you unique!

Once when I was sitting in a panel discussion about my life, I shared with participants and observers, some of them superintendents, my failures and the number of times I failed and had to get back up again. Many of them didn't have to go through as many failures as I did. But I talked about getting up again and that life has a way of knocking us down sometimes. We also have to recognize that sometimes we get knocked down so hard that it's really hard to get back up, and I understand that.

There are people whom you know that have habits or perhaps you have habits, and those habits have a way of keeping you down. And those habits have ripple effects throughout many areas of your life. It could be relationships, the way you relate to people, and habits that influence outcomes and many other aspects of your life. Some of us have seen people in hardship and wonder how that person got there. You see others sitting and reading or you think of a friend and wonder how that person ever ended up in a particular situation. Now, I can relate to and have friends who can relate to these thoughts. But one powerful tool for success is a simple and very profound principle. If you say you are going to be all right, that's the gift of getting back up again. That's a gift and an amazing secret to success. When you get knocked down, get back up, and keep moving forward. And when you are fully aware that everyone gets knocked down, you are going to feel the hurt of other people's choices as they come crashing down on you. Some of these bombs will be dropped unexpectantly: your parents' divorce, a family member dies, or failing to graduate can knock you down in an instant.

Going to school can be hard, living in certain homes can be hard, avoiding gangs can be hard, losing friendships can be hard, losing loved ones can be hard, knowing which way to turn can be hard – all ultimately involves getting from under a great cloud of despair. But I'm here to tell you to hold on and never give up. Don't close your eyes. The light will break through the clouds as it always does. When you step out from under defeat and bounce back from life's hard blows, you'll come back stronger than before. **#strongerthanever**. I'm asking that you hold on.

Get back up when you get knocked down and move forward. Keep moving forward but steady yourself for the next hit because it will come. That's life. The next hit may not knock you to the ground, but you're actually going to be stronger and have fortitude from the hits that you've already taken. Now if you get knocked down the next time, you already know the process – don't despair and get back up again. It's always worth fighting for. There is always hope at the end of the tunnel. Remember: It *ain't* about how hard you get hit; it's about how hard you can get hit and keep moving forward. Isn't that awesome? Remember the story I shared about applying for a job 18 times before I finally got called for the job in Halifax. When I got the call, I was ecstatic because it was awesome and I loved it! That's how winners keep winning!

Key #10: Honor Your Parents

Some cultures around the world, especially in continents like Asia, uphold the value of honoring the mother and father. There is value within those cultures that honoring elderly figures is an expectation. In America, I have seen that honoring your mother and father is a concept that is basically nonexistent. And we only celebrate honoring our parents on two days – Mother's Day and Father's Day.

I have come to understand that we have been instructed to honor our mother and father. It is so much bigger than us. It is the fabric of who we are as Americans. So, when we are told to honor our elders, our mothers and fathers, it isn't a choice we make or something we do when we feel like it; instead, it is a direct command from a higher being. And when you look at this, you see it very clearly, so I need you to listen up because this concept is tied to your blessings in the future. I'm going to give you three reasons why you should value this key more than any of the other keys that I have given you.

The *first reason* that you should honor your parents is extremely profound: Honoring your parents honors you <u>and</u> honors your Creator. When we look at the act of creation and how you got here, we have to recognize that it comes from a power much stronger than us. And when you honor your mother and father, you are honoring Creation itself. There were times in my life when I didn't feel like honoring my parents, but it wasn't a choice: HONORING MY PARENTS HONORS CREATION. That alone should give you the motivation that you need. It's cool to think that as we show simple gestures of kindness and respect to our parents by helping them around the house, paying them a compliment or telling them how much we appreciate them, we are actually honoring the Creator. When you do things in such a way that make them smile and laugh, as opposed to crying and feeling depressed, you are actually honoring the Creation – the Creator Himself.

The **second reason** for honoring your parents is because they simply deserve it. They deserve it. I remember saying this when I was growing up: "I'm not going to do it." And I can understand why you might be tempted to say, "I'm not going to honor my parents, they didn't do a good job raising me." "They don't deserve my respect." "Daddy, he left me when I was young." "Mom, she didn't buy me everything I wanted for Christmas. She was neglectful in a lot of ways." Maybe your father was an alcoholic and your mother did everything she could, but she was very young at the time she had you. There are a lot reasons as to why you could feel hurt about the treatment you feel you have been given. I got it – trust me. I get it but that's not what you are supposed to do. Honoring your parents is not a condition, it is an EXPECTATION: Honor your mother and father PERIOD. It doesn't say, 'Honor your mother and father only if they are honorable.' That's not what it says. Honor your mother and father, period – regardless of whether their actions may sometimes be dishonorable, just as your actions may sometimes be dishonorable, but because they are your parents. That's reason enough for you to respect them. There are no loopholes. You have to submit to this requirement.

For example, both of my parents dropped out of school in Birmingham, Alabama, in the sixth grade. My father goes off and fights two tours in Vietnam; my mother cleaned homes on the weekends and worked during the holiday period so we could have clothes and gifts during those special times during the year. I'm deeply appreciative, but they worked sometimes 12-15-hour days providing food, clothes and shelter for me. And I bring home all D's on my report card. Now, my father and mother dropped out of school in the sixth grade and they are providing for six kids. I never missed a meal. I never had dirty clothes, and yet I'm turning around and bringing home 6 D's, when I have a bed to sleep, I have not missed a meal, I have clothes – I have everything I need – and I am not performing well in school. I want you to think about that.

Look at your grades. Are your grades bringing honor to your parents? Are your behaviors bringing honor to your parents? When you look at what they are giving you, even though you feel it is not enough, it's still better than what they had. And how are you showing appreciation for their sacrifices every day? Are you giving them the accolades that they deserve? Those accolades should come in the forms of actions – your report card, perfect attendance, leadership awards, playing extracurricular sports, your contributing to a team, your work on the side, bringing earned money home . . . There are so many ways, so many actions— cleaning up around the house, taking out the trash, cutting the grass—that will bring your family honor.

The **third reason** to honor your mother and father is so that, as it says in the Bible, your days will be long. That's a promise of a blessing. That's a benefit or a reward. Honoring your parents will result in the blessing of a longer life and that you may be well-off in your life. This is how you tap into that type of good fortune. When you can see these things in your life, they are being unmistakably displayed. *For nothing is secret, that shall not be manifested.* Manifest those blessings in your life by tapping into the actions of honoring your mother and father. These insights are not only important but _extremely important_.

I want to take some time to ask some questions that I want you to reflect on:

1. What is your view of honor?
2. Have you been living with a proper understanding of honoring your mother and your father?
3. Do you have any bitterness or unforgiveness toward your mom and dad that might be keeping you from honoring them properly?

4. When was the last time you really honored your mother and your father?
5. In what ways can you practice honoring them on a regular basis?

**Stop honoring your parents only
On Mother's Day and Father's Day.
Honor your parents daily!
Honor your parents throughout your life!**

Key #11: Stop Blaming Your Parents

I had to learn that to my friends, complaining about my parents was pathetic and pointless. While I was sitting there complaining about my parents, my friends were probably ignoring me and my complaints were more likely annoying to them. To be completely honest with myself, I had to get sick of all the whining and all the complaining as well as my anger, my victim mentality, and my inability to see what my current attitude did, not what my dad did or what my mother did. I had to see that my inability and my current attitude were actually my biggest problem. So, I had to actually become sick of blaming my bad behavior on my parents.

What was standing between me and success was me. It wasn't my dad, it wasn't my history – it was me. And it was the fact that I walked around thinking that my parents sabotaged my life and that they were responsible for my detrimental situation. Isn't that crazy? My then-current stupid behaviors, grades, and less than desirable outcomes were all just evidence of my immaturity and how much in denial I was. I was actually delusional. Yes, we all get that way sometimes. Sometimes our childhoods are tough. Guess what – Welcome to the World's Greatest Club. Because every time I talk with my friends about their childhood, they say the same thing, too.

The first year when we moved to the projects and to government housing, my mother told me I wasn't going to get anymore Christmas gifts. I thought she was joking. But she actually meant it. I woke up on Christmas morning and didn't get any gifts. My brothers and sisters got gifts because they were younger than me, but I got nothing, so I started playing the victim, until I went downstairs and saw my friends. Guess what – they didn't get anything either. I then realized that I was not alone. My mother was doing everything she could do just to provide for us: buy food and clothing – I got that. Sometimes my mom didn't let me use her car to go to work or go to class. I thought that was extremely selfish on her part, but guess what – stuff happens, so let us be honest. Some parents aren't doing what they are supposed to but most are and, YES, many of us have been hurt physically, emotionally, and psychologically by our parents.

I'm not suggesting that you deny your parents. That is not what I'm saying. What I am suggesting is that you don't live in the past. I had to learn that misery loves company. It will kill you and it will kill you in so many different ways if you live in the past, blaming your history or your presence. No matter how much you think your parents deserve your anger, your resentment, or your hostility, I'm telling you it serves no positive purpose. First, it will hurt you more than you think; secondly, it will stop you from being a big, immature baby. You need to stop! I needed to stop being a big, stupid baby and finally realize that I was responsible for my current reality. No matter what my dad or my mother may have done, or did not do, I was responsible for my current reality.

You may have very good reason to be eternally ticked off at your folks. I'm saying, "Let it go." You may have the best reason in the world, but let it go anyway. I want you to move on. And it is not about what they do or don't deserve, it's about what you deserve. If you want to destroy your potential, your enthusiasm, your optimism, your hope, then become a chronic blamer and blame everything on your past and your parents. Hang on to that hurt. Stay right there enjoying that misery because you know that you'll stay right where you are. Or you could listen to me and let me save you some serious time. And just believe when I tell you that blaming others is a pointless, destructive, pathetic waste of your potential and emotional energy. If you are not careful, you are going to waste your whole life blaming others. It can destroy you from the inside out.

You know you can actually die of bitter resentment and a tortured soul because you never found a way to let go of that self-perpetuated hatred of yourself and your family. Again, misery loves company. Why are you desperately holding on to emotional garbage of years ago? It's you that's the problem. And you are going to be 25, 35, 50, 55 and you're still going to be thinking, talking, and behaving like the teenager you were in high school. You need to wake up, and you need to wake up now!

The only thing you can change about your past is how you are responding to it now. THE ONLY THING YOU CAN CHANGE ABOUT YOUR PAST IS HOW YOU ARE RESPONDING TO IT NOW.
So, I really want you to learn to let go. You cannot go around blaming, for example, why you don't like the police, why you have poor communication skills, or why you can't keep a relationship – all destructive habits. Add to those additional destructive thoughts and actions: the violent behaviors, the way you feel about yourself, the way your body looks, your poor eating habits, what your parents did or didn't do. You are capable of independent thought – you can make your own decisions. You can choose your own behaviors and be responsible for your own existence. Can't you? So, choose to create a different world for yourself.

Perhaps your parents taught you how to be, but it may be that your parents taught you how not to be. That is what my parents taught me: how not to be. I totally understand that your parents were not always complete in what they should or could have been for you, the child: caring, supportive, forgiving, understanding, loving, available, honest, etc. And I'm sorry, but I want you to know that you are not alone. You are in a large majority. The problem with parents is that they are flawed, just like we all are. None of us are perfect and you'll realize that when you become a parent yourself. Blaming your parents is a slippery slope of self- pity. It's self-destructive behavior and it doesn't do you any good. Just Stop! Move on!

Key #12: Innovate, Don't Imitate

There were times in my life when I wished I had looked like someone else. I wished I had hair like someone else. I wished I could run and jump or play basketball like someone else. I wished my body looked like someone else's. You may think that imitation is the greatest form of flattery and you might feel it's necessary to imitate someone you actually admire. But what I had learned was that as I was focused on imitating someone, I was actually hindering my creativity and innovation. Why is that? It was because I was starting to be what someone else wanted me to be, instead of what my inner voice was telling me to be.

Innovation and creativity are the leaping off points to success. What I had learned was that when I allowed myself to be myself, I was much more creative and much more disciplined to meet my goals. So, what I'm asking you to do is to look at the other people as leaping off points. You might want to play basketball like Michael Jordan, but you will end up being like yourself, so you will look at moves like Michael Jordan had performed and then you would adopt the moves into your arsenal, but you will also be able to add your own creative twist to make it uniquely yours because no two people are made the same.

So, what inspires you? When we look at creativity and innovation, you have to look at inspiration and what actually inspires you. I had an opportunity to meet some kids, some students, who wanted to have their own step team. They wanted one started at their school, but they had no direction, no clue, and no resources to becoming a step team. I asked them why they were interested in wanting a step team. I challenged them to go out and study how to create a step team and to make a list of requirements for having a step team in school. They went out, they had meetings with folks, they recruited their own coach, and they talked about how they felt when they were working together as a team in unison stepping and how good it felt and how they were able to express themselves through their moves. I was impressed. And as their superintendent, I went out and got funds for them to have their step team. But I was impressed with their energy and passion. You see, when you are innovative and creative, your energy becomes contagious.

I was so impressed with their innovation, energy and passion that I even got up and tried the steps with them. It was awesome. So, you have to ask yourself what inspires you, where is it that you are trying to go? What puts a smile on your face? As a superintendent, or even as a teacher on the job, I was always looking for ideas to try to move myself forward in my profession. I was always searching. The reason I was searching was because I didn't think I had any good ideas within myself, so I was constantly looking for outside sources instead of speaking from my own heart. I actually thought I needed to use other ideas that were good because I wasn't a very creative person. And I wasn't able to be creative myself, so over time, I had to shift my own thinking about myself and own my own ideas and what I knew how to do. When I would find a good idea, I needed to not mess with it; so overtime, I shifted my ideas because I wasn't really respecting my own creativity. Often, I would find a good idea and wouldn't mess with it. I wasn't comfortable with my creativity and allowing myself to be innovative. Mostly, this came from repeated failures that I had experienced. I buried those failures inside myself and started telling myself that I wasn't a very creative or innovative person. Instead of seeing each of these opportunities as learning opportunities that could allow me to be even more creative and innovative, I would see them as weights that kept me from excelling.

By using other people's ideas, what I was saying was that I was not proud of myself and that I did not believe I was a creative or innovative person. In some ways, this can wear you down over time to the point where you become robotic and you are only doing what other people tell you to do. Because inside yourself, you're saying, *I cannot think for myself.* And I'm here to tell you that you can think for yourself. You can think for yourself and you MUST think for yourself. Because inside of me, I've noticed that there was always a nagging beat in my chest that was always reminding me that there was so much more to me than I was letting out.

Eventually, that beat in my chest, grew in intensity and one day in a bold move, I decided to try out a few of my own ideas and instead of planning like they would fail, I began to plan for success. And this was a major turning point in my career. I had applied for the superintendence 18 times before I finally got the call to the Halifax schools. But every time up to 18, I was going in as the person I thought they wanted me to be, not as the person that Eric Cunningham actually is. So, for eighteen times I was thinking of other people and I was actually imitating them and going in like them, dressing like them, and losing the job. I began to realize that until I began to be myself and act like myself I was not going to be able to emerge as the best candidate and win the job. I had to be innovative and let my creativity show and shine. Inspiration is one need you must have in order to be successful today. All of us are full of wonder. All of us are full of questions, yet we hold those questions for later. We do not ask those questions because we feel they may be viewed as stupid or dumb questions. And we don't want people to laugh at us. We do just enough to get through. But I'm here to tell you that it is your responsibility to release the scholar that is inside of you and to stand proud being the person that you are.

Remember the story that I told you about the desk and how I had to sit down at that desk and study, and even though a paper earned an F+, I would continue to study. That F+ turned into a D- But it was my work. And the D- turned into a C-, but it was still my work. And then a C- turned into a C+. It was still my work. And a C+ turned into a B-. Still my work until I ended up becoming Dr. Cunningham, owning my own work. I'm here to tell you that through innovation, you will grow and you will eventually become the man or the woman that you were meant to be because we are all creative and innovative in some way.

Key #13: Be Like Water

I love a quote by Bruce Lee. I grew up watching old karate, Kung Fu movies and the person I most loved watching was Bruce Lee. He had this quote that he taught his students and he promoted the idea of being like water. His quote is: "Be like water, making its way through cracks. Do not be assertive but adjust to the object and you shall find a way around or through it. If nothing within you stays rigid, outward things would disclose themselves. Empty your mind; be formless, shapeless, like water. If you put it in a cup, it becomes a cup. You put water into a bottle, it becomes the bottle. If you put water in a teapot, it becomes the teapot. Now water can flow or it can crash. Be water, my friend."
–Bruce Lee

When I think about living, and when I think about what Lee is saying, I tend to watch water and how it flows. Actually, it looks so beautiful as it goes over the rocks, but it can also be extremely dangerous because it can actually hide its depths and all the dangers that may be lurking beneath the surface. When you think of your life and live it like water, you will be able to flow through situations, the cracks that come through your life. You don't have to be assertive, but you have to learn to adjust to the object and flow around it. If nothing within you stays rigid, outward things will disclose themselves. So, if you can adapt to the circumstances that you find yourself in, and you do not become rigid and hard, a solution will emerge that will show you a pathway around them.

When Lee talks about emptying your mind, he talks about being without form. When you look at yourself without form or being shapeless, you become much more fluid and agile, AND you can respond to any situation that you may find yourself in. So, if you find yourself making poor grades and you flow like water, you will be able to adapt to the reason why you received those poor grades and work your way up step by step.

113

When I started embracing the concept of living like water, I was able to find myself much more flexible and adaptable to the situations that I found myself facing every day. All of the situations that you find yourself in is nothing but life. It's just life. Life will throw you many curves, but if you respond like water, and you adjust to the circumstance that you find yourself in, you will always find your way around it. This will ALWAYS be the case because the path will disclose itself to you. And whatever situations that you find yourself in you will be able to reform yourself and reinvent yourself in such a way that it actually works and you actually become the solution.

So, the concept of water promotes agility and flexibility. You are also able to create a strategy, a solution to find your way around the problem.

Key #14: Grow a Good Life

Throughout my life, I have always had to understand the process of improvement. There is the process that you have to embrace as you strive for a much better life. And it is a process that I want you to enjoy.

I want you to enjoy the JOURNEY of growth. When I talk about growing a better life, I want you to know that you have to talk about pursuing your dreams. It all begins with your dreams and then PURSUING your dreams. The verb "pursue" is an active verb. That means you have to go for it! And that's a daily effort —yesterday doesn't count. All that matters is what you are doing today! You have to grow your dreams as you live your life like water. As you become powerful, adaptable, and gentle, your dreams will also change. But your true dream in life is to have a long, healthy and happy life regardless of your job, regardless of the school, and regardless of all of the rewards that life will bring you. With all of these things, you will always be pursuing something else. Once you reach one destination, you are going to want to go somewhere else. And that's natural.

But when you focus on growing a good life, you are now sharpening your attention to focus and that focus will bring persistence and patience. You will learn to LISTEN. I had to learn to listen. I especially had to learn to listen with my eyes ... look at the person who was speaking to me. I learned to listen with my eyes when I was playing college basketball: my coach would always tell us to LOOK at him. I didn't quite understand what he meant at that time until I began to focus. When you look at someone while they are talking, you are now focusing on the person who is communicating with you. And when you focus, you can actually listen. That is called ACTIVE LISTENING. That is needed as you grow. Subsequently, you focus on doing the work. Then, after you are focused, don't dwell on making mistakes. Just do the work. You're going to make mistakes while you are working and that's okay. MISTAKES ARE OPPORTUNITIES FOR GROWTH. I always want you to *try* to do your work; when you try, you are practicing and getting better. EVERYTIME YOU TRY, YOU ARE PRACTICING. When we are talking about growing our life, we are talking about doing the work. The work might be laden with mistakes. You may be taking a class in math that is boring. I had a hard time with theorems in geometry. I could not understand that concept. I had to go over and over and over and over the information again and again and again until I began to figure it out. My brain adapted and I began to figure it out. But you have to do the work! You have to try, even if the first of many efforts are failures.

Remember that I applied to be a superintendent eighteen times before I was awarded the opportunity to be Superintendent in Halifax County schools. Eighteen times! Oftentimes, when you strike out that many times, you begin to think: Is this job for me? Am I ready to do this job? Do I have the 'stuff' that's needed to be a good superintendent? After you have struck out so many times, it is important to CONTINUE TO DO THE WORK. As I continued to do the work and to strive; I began to get rid of useless distractions. I began to minimize those distractions because I became more focused on obtaining a specific goal.

Again, when we talk about growing your life, we are talking about doing the things that will allow you to live a good life. And that is a journey to self-sufficiency.

Key #15: Focus On Literacy

The dictionary defines literacy as the ability to read and write. A more detailed definition includes the ability to identify, understand, interpret, create, communicate and compute. It also encompasses the ability to express thoughts, feelings and ideas. Literacy will provide levels of proficiency necessary to function on a job, in the family, in the community and in society.

The reason I would like Key #15 to focus on literacy is because all of us need to focus on the ability to identify, understand, interpret, create and communicate, as well as express thoughts, feelings and ideas. Once we are able to do that, we will be able to effectively live in our society. Literacy is part of everyday life. Words, written or spoken, are used to communicate our ideas and feelings with each other. Everything we do – EVERYTHING we do – involves reading and writing and, to a lesser degree, mathematics. Throughout this book I talked about how I improved my reading and my writing, as well as my mathematical ability, in order to become Dr. C. You see, I believe that the **ability to read** is fundamentally important. It is the **foundation of success.**

I am sure everyone knows the expression, *Reading is Fundamental.* Why is that so? What does it mean? In today's world, reading is necessary to understand your emails, the Internet, text messages, viewing television programs, videos, computers, video games, job applications, transportation, descriptions, directions, driving, etc. You get the idea . . . these are just a few, for the list is endless.

There are worthwhile benefits to literacy. Students with strong, well-developed literacy skills are less likely to drop out of school and are less likely to be involved in crime. But literacy is just not the ability to read and write words. That is a common misconception held by many. Importantly, it is the ability to comprehend the words spoken and written. The ability to comprehend words as you read them is a skill that many of our students – many of you (and I was one of them) and some adults – face every day. Failure to comprehend the words before you can be extremely frustrating and cause feelings of low self-esteem, poor grades in school and embarrassment. I know how that feels because I have experienced those feelings.

I want to go back to when I failed fourth grade. (I talked about that earlier in the book.) When I failed the fourth grade, I was held back because of my inability to read...I thought I could read: I could read simple books, but, again, I could not comprehend. And that inability kept me from being promoted to the fifth grade. When you are held back and your friends are ahead of you, you are embarrassed, you are ashamed. And then you learn to play smart. Do you know what I mean when I say "play smart"? In actuality, *you act like you know but you don't.* You just don't. You read the first couple of words in a paragraph, you don't finish the entire page or chapter, and then you really try to adlib and pretend that you know. You become very defensive when someone questions you because you actually don't know and you are afraid to tell them that you don't know. It is because you can't read—you can't comprehend what you are trying to read. That begins the cycle of what I call "playing smart." I want you not to play smart. I want everyone to BE smart. So, we have to transition from PLAYING to BEING! (Keep in mind as we think about transitioning that throughout this book, there has been a focus on moving from *playing* to *being.*)

According to statistics from the National Assessment of Adult Literacy (NAAL), approximately 14 percent of adults in North Carolina lack basic prose literacy skills. These adults experience reading and writing difficulties that seriously affect their daily lives and that of their families. The National Assessment of Educational Progress Scores for 2015 reports that 62% of North Carolina's 4th graders are below proficiency in reading. The national score is 65%. Research indicates that fourth grade is the benchmark. Fourth graders who are reading below grade level are 7% less likely to catch up to their grade level. I want you to think about that. That's how important reading is. And reading was a barrier for me. I want you to see the cycle that follows from your inability to read, write, and comprehend. So, let's work on that.

I have a friend whose nephew Brian cried every night at the age of three because he could not read. Sure, he had many books and looked at them daily. The pictures were nice, but he could not read the words. One day my friend visited her sister and there was Brian with his books. He was reading as he turned the pages. She was amazed and she said to her sister, "I didn't know Brian could read." To which the sister replied, "Brian cannot read but decided that he would create his own story from the pictures in the book." And he read his books from his story creations.

Some of you may laugh, but when I think about that story, I think it is actually brilliant! You see, *when you want something so bad, you will find a way to make it happen.* And Brian wanted to read. When Brian did learn to read, with the assistance from special tutors and his mother, he had two stories to read: the actual words in the book and the ones he had created.

Reading can take you to many levels. It can develop the mind and take you to creative places that you never thought were possible. So, let's suppose we could clone Brian, 62%. That's the below proficiency reading level for 4th graders. You follow me, okay. Maybe that's a little high – that's reaching. But suppose we could clone Brian 50%. Suppose there were 50% of students who were that motivated to learn to read, that they would cry at night because they wanted to read so badly. Suppose we could provide intervention programs like tutoring to increase reading abilities at an early age. Would this make a difference? I strongly believe the answer is "yes."

The emphasis on literacy must start at the beginning of your journey into education. From kindergarten to third grade, you learn to read. From 4th grade to 12th grade and throughout your life, you read to learn. REMEMBER THAT! So now you understand why reading is so important. I will not attempt to list all the reasons reading is so important; however, I will give you FIVE REASONS that reading is a vital skill to strive for in everyday life from children, to teenagers, to adults.

REASON ONE:
Reading is fundamental to function in today's society. However, it is important to realize that just because you are struggling with basic reading skills is not a sign of low intelligence. *Just because you are having difficulty reading, it is not a sign of low intelligence.* Don't believe that hype. Many highly intelligent people have poor reading skills, but when properly taught, the handicaps (difficulties) can be erased. And with determination and hard work, you or anyone can accomplish good reading and comprehension skills. I am a living testimony of that.

REASON TWO:
Reading is important because it develops the mind. Understanding written words is one way the mind grows. Learning to read at an early age will help you develop your language skills and it will also help you learn to listen.

REASON THREE:
Reading is important because it is how we discover new things. There are many learning tools in today's society: books, magazines, the Internet, etc. require the ability to read. We live in a world of unlimited information, and reading is the best way to take advantage and grace all areas of education.

REASON FOUR:
Reading develops imagination and creativity. I want you to remember Brian. Not only did he learn to read, but he learned

to create. He learned to write because he used his imagination to create his own stories. Brian is a Superstar!

REASON FIVE:
Reading helps expand one's vocabulary. Reading new words can create a better understanding of word usage and definitions for immediate or later use.

In conclusion, *I believe that the joy of reading is powerful.* I wish you prosperity. I wish you much success. I wish that this book will allow you to grow in understanding yourself as well as your passions and what drives you.

I want you to remember that you're NOT here by accident: YOU ARE HERE FOR A REASON. "The two important dates," Mark Twain said, "are not your sunrise and your sunset. It's the day you were born and the day you find out why."

Good Luck!

References

Augustine Literacy Project. (2016). *Facts and figures.* Retrieved from www.augustineproject.org/facts-figures.html/

Guest, E. A. (1921). *Don't quit.* Retrieved from http://www.all-creatures.org/discuss/dontquit-10120810-k.html

Lee, B.. (1971). Be *like water.* Retrieved from https://www.brainpicking.org/2013/05/29/like-water-Bruce-lee-artist-of-life/

Lombardi, V. (n.d.). *Winners never quit.* Retrieved from http://www.1000ventures.com/business_guide/crosscuttings/quotes_authors_lombardi.html

Masser, M., & Creed.L. (1986). *The greatest love of all: A Whitney-Houston soundtrack.* Retrieved from https://genius.com/Whitney-houston-greatest-love-of-all-lyrics/

National Assessment of Educational Progress.(2015). Sobering *statistics.* Retrieved from http://www. National reportcard.gov/reading_math_g12_2015/#/

National Center for Education Statistics. (2003). *What is NAAL?* Retrieved from http://nces.ed.gov/naal/

Random Acts of Kindness Ideas. Retrieved from http://www.randomactsofkindness.org

APPENDIX A
YOUNG CHAMPIONS GUIDE TO EXCELLENCE
#LetsGetStarted

By reading this book you have demonstrated the desire to change your life. So far, this book has provided you with a new set of tools to rebuild your life. Now that you have the tools, what are you going to do with them? Now is the time to begin the process of charting a new course to 5-star living.

It has been said that the distance between dreams and reality is called an ACTION PLAN. In order to achieve that 5-star dream, all young champions need an action plan. An action plan is the pathway you will take to accomplish your dreams. For example, when you take a trip you don't just jump into the car and drive. You make a plan, you set your destination, and you take care of the needed steps to make your trip a success.

During your life, you will have countless dreams, many hopes and desires, and tons of goals. This is your first stair step. The question is how you will turn your dreams, hopes, desires and goals into real life accomplishments as you climb the stairway of life. The answer is a guide with specific details on how you will get to the top. An action plan will provide you with a road map to start climbing your staircase to success, build goals, and create opportunities from failures. An action plan will allow you to evaluate, re-evaluate your goals and outcomes and then climb to the next step with *new* goals, opportunities and outcomes until you reach the top.

Your action plan will revolve around your mastery of the 3 R's: Readiness, Respectfulness, and Resiliency. Listed below are the artifacts that you need to master each area. Pay attention to each point and apply them to your everyday life. You need to make a conscious effort to apply each bullet. I want you to remember to be easy on yourself. This is new and you might find it frustrating at times, especially when your efforts are not received positively by other people. Young Champions, let's get started.

STARTING FROM THE BOTTOM WORKBOOK

BE YOUR BEST CHAMPION

This book was designed to provide a course for young champions to navigate and become successful. The following workbook will allow champions to embrace personal goals and develop self-esteem. Focus on being positive and think of yourself as gifted and talented. You can accomplish whatever you put your mind to if you want it bad enough!

YOU ARE A WINNER!!

Now is the time to begin the process of charting a new course to 5- star living.

Re-invent yourself and become a better version of yourself.

NEVER QUIT!!!

CHAMPIONS WORKBOOK

1. List three of your current goals and what they mean to you.

_____

_____

_____

_____

_____

_____

_____

_____

_____

2. What are your plans for improving your grades and your Grade Point Average (GPA)?

_____

_____

_____

_____

_____

_____

_____

_____

_____

3. What does it mean to re-invent yourself?

_____

_____

_____

_____

_____

_____

_____

_____

_____

_____

4. What happens when you reach the top level of your staircase?

_____

_____

_____

_____

_____

_____

_____

_____

_____

_____

_____

5. Why is it so important to believe in yourself?

_____

_____

_____

_____

_____

_____

_____

_____

_____

_____

6. Who are the "dream stealers" in your life and what do they say about you?

_____

_____

_____

_____

_____

_____

_____

_____

_____

_____

7. What can you do or say to show the "dream stealers" that they don't know you and that you aren't willing to play their game?

_____

_____

_____

_____

_____

_____

_____

_____

8. Is there someone who has been a positive mentor in your life? Who was that person, and explain the connection to you?

_____

_____

_____

_____

_____

_____

_____

_____

_____

9. What is character? Why is character important?

_____

_____

_____

_____

_____

_____

_____

_____

_____

10. Integrity is having strong moral principles and values. List five reasons why integrity is important when climbing your stair steps to success.

_____

_____

_____

_____

_____

_____

_____

_____

_____

11. Why is it important to be polite?

_____

_____

_____

_____

_____

_____

_____

_____

_____

_____

12. If you see your friends being disrespectful, do you speak up? What do you say?

_____

_____

_____

_____

_____

_____

_____

_____

_____

13. How do you study? Describe your special place to study?

_____

_____

_____

_____

_____

_____

_____

_____

_____

_____

14. What does work ethic mean to you?

_____

_____

_____

_____

_____

_____

_____

_____

_____

_____

15. How can you demonstrate a positive work ethic at school?

_____

_____

_____

_____

_____

_____

_____

_____

_____

16. How can you use the 3 R's - Readiness, Respectfulness, and Resiliency - in creating a strong work ethic?

_____

_____

_____

_____

_____

_____

_____

_____

_____

17. What are you afraid might happen if you fail?

_____

_____

_____

_____

_____

_____

_____

_____

_____

_____

18. What actions can you take to "push past fear?"

_____

_____

_____

_____

_____

_____

_____

_____

_____

_____

19. Who can you ask to support you to "push past fear and help you reach your goals?"

_____

_____

_____

_____

_____

_____

_____

_____

_____

20. How do you get back up when you fall down?

_____

_____

_____

_____

_____

_____

_____

_____

_____

_____

21. Create your Winning Game! (#youareachampion)

You are in the game and have one shot! How will you make it work for you? What will you do to achieve your goal and become a champion? Using the 3 R concept (Readiness, Respectfulness, Resiliency), create a winning game designed to help you reach your goals. Remember: You are positive! You are great! You are a Winner! You are a Champion

My name is:

_____

The name of my game is:

_____

The key players in my winning game are:

_____
_____
_____
_____
_____

Five or more rules (goals) of my game are:

_____

_____

_____

_____

_____

_____

_____

_____

_____

_____

_____

_____

Five or more steps I will take to be successful in my game are:

_____

_____

_____

_____

_____

_____

_____

_____

_____

_____

List five or more people you will ask to support you and the reason(s) why.

_____

_____

_____

_____

_____

_____

_____

_____

_____

_____

If I fall down during the game, the steps I will take to get back up are:

_____

_____

_____

_____

_____

_____

_____

_____

_____

_____

Appendix B
A Message to Parents/Guardians

I have always loved children. The education of children has been my passion and my priority for most of my life. Children and their well-being are the drive, the motivation, the devoted commitment for everything that I have done and will continue to do in the future.

This book was written for young adults as a guide to re-invent their lives and motivate them to become better students. By sharing my experiences and goals to reaching my current position as School Superintendent, I have provided tools that your child (along with your support) can use to chart a new course. All dreams are possible for young champions who dream big, work hard and are constantly resilient.

There are many ways you can play an active role in your child's education, both at home and at school. I encourage you to monitor your child's school work, communicate with teachers, visit their classrooms and volunteer your time. At home, I strongly suggest that you encourage reading, help develop healthy habits, ask questions, listen carefully, offer encouragement and make an effort each day to spend quality time together.

The lyrics from one of my favorite songs, "The Greatest Love of All," by the late Whitney Houston give me inspiration to continue my journey to enhance the lives of children.

> *"I believe children are our future*
> *Teach them well and let them lead the way*
> *Show them all the beauty they possess inside*
> *Give them a sense of pride to make it easier"*

Dr. Eric L. Cunningham, Superintendent
Halifax County School District, Halifax County, North Carolina

About the Author

Dr. Eric Cunningham (Dr. "C") is the current Superintendent of Halifax County Schools. He strongly believes that his responsibility is to lead by example as he strives to provide guidance, motivation and, protection in pursuit of excellence to the greatest and most important assets of Halifax County: Our Children. He has dedicated his entire career to supporting and improving the lives of not just children in schools, but communities in which they live. Dr. Cunningham is committed to the old school philosophy that "it takes a village to raise a child".

Eric L. Cunningham is from Birmingham, Alabama, and relocated to Virginia in his early adolescent years. His hunger and desire for education led him to achieve a Bachelor of Science degree and Master of Arts degree in Counselling from Liberty University. He also obtained a Doctorate degree in Administration and Supervision from the University of Virginia.

Dr. Cunningham has over 25 years of educating children and serving the community. Prior to his appointment as Superintendent, he served as Associate Superintendent for Administration and Operations for Nash-Rocky Mount Public Schools in North Carolina. Additionally, he served as Assistant Superintendent for Administration in Caroline County Public Schools in Virginia and as Director of Human Resources for Spotsylvania County Public Schools in Fredericksburg, Virginia. Dr. Cunningham has clearly worn many hats during his career, and has many accomplishments, but it is his character and his integrity that are most impressive and are without doubt, recognized in his leadership.

Dr. Cunningham has served on many boards including: Board of Directors for the Halifax County Chamber of Commerce, Big Brothers and Big Sisters, the Red Cross, and the North Carolina

PTA. Throughout his career, Dr. Cunningham has earned leadership awards, including the Administrator of the Year for Nash Rocky Mount Public School, but he is most appreciative of the ones that directly benefit teachers and children such as the Appreciation Award from the Boys and Girls Club, the Appreciation Award from the American Association of School Personnel Administrators for creating an Outstanding Mentor Teacher Program and the Adult Achiever Award for being an outstanding role model.

Halifax County students call him Dr. C and Dr. C has an amazing vision for Halifax County School students. His primary focus and priority is to make learning "contagious", not only in the classroom but throughout the district. His message to everyone is simple, yet sincere: "Strive to be the Best". Halifax County Schools will not just show children the path to success, but will walk beside them, embracing them, encouraging them and educating them for the future.

Halifax County School Superintendent: Dr. Eric L. Cunningham - Spiritual Servant, Devoted Father, Teacher, Counselor, Mentor, Educational Administrator, Highly Skilled Organizer, Community Leader, Motivational Speaker and above all –Advocate for Children.

Made in the USA
Middletown, DE
01 March 2019